AMAZON
WEB
SERVICES

Functional And Complete Guide
For Beginners. Amazon Business
Philosophy: Having A Full
Understanding To AWS

DOUGLAS DAHANNE

In no way is it legal to reproduce, duplicate, or transmit any part of this document in either electronic means or in printed format. Recording of this publication is strictly prohibited and any storage of this document is not allowed unless with written permission from the publisher. All rights reserved

The information provided herein is stated to be truthful and consistent, in that any liability, in terms of inattention or otherwise, by any usage or abuse of any policies, processes, or directions contained within is the solitary and utter responsibility of the recipient reader. Under no circumstances will any legal responsibility or blame be held against the publisher for any reparation, damages, or monetary loss due to the

DISCLAIMER

The information contained within this eBook is strictly for educational purposes. If you wish to apply ideas contained in this eBook, you are taking full responsibility for your actions.

The author has made every effort to ensure the accuracy of the information within this book was correct at time of publication. The author does not assume and hereby disclaims any liability to any party for any loss, damage, or disruption caused by errors or omissions, whether such errors or omissions result from accident, negligence, or any other cause.

Table of Contents

INTRODUCTION

Amazon Web Services (AWS) is a comprehensive, developing cloud computing platform provided by Amazon. It gives a blend of framework as a help (IaaS), stage as a service (PaaS) and bundled programming as a service (SaaS) contributions.

Amazon Web Services (AWS) is the market pioneer in IaaS (Infrastructure-as-a-Service) and PaaS (Platform-as-a-Service) for cloud ecosystems, which can be combined to create a versatile cloud application without stressing about delays related to framework provisioning (figure, storage, and network) and management.

With AWS you can select the explicit solutions you need, and just pay for exactly what you use, resulting in lower capital expenditure and faster time to value without sacrificing application performance or user experience.

AWS launched in 2006 from the interior infrastructure that Amazon.com built to handle its online retail tasks. AWS was one of the first organizations to present a pay-as-you-go cloud computing model that scales to give users with figure, storage or throughput as required.

Amazon Web Services provides services from dozens of server farms spread across accessibility zones (AZs) in regions across the world. An AZ represents a location that regularly contains multiple physical data centers, while a region is a collection of

AZs in geographic proximity connected by low-latency arrange links. An AWS customer can turn up virtual machines (VMs) and replicate information in various AZs to accomplish a highly reliable infrastructure that is impervious to disappointments of individual servers or a whole server farm.

New and existing companies can build their digital framework partially or entirely in the cloud with AWS, making the on-premise information center a thing of the past. The AWS cloud guarantees infrastructure reliability, compliance with security standards, and the capacity to instantly grow or shrivel your infrastructure to meet your needs and amplify your budget, all without upfront investment in equipment.

More than 100 services involve the Amazon Web Services portfolio, including those for compute, databases, framework the board, application development and security. These services, by category, include:

EC2: Server setup and facilitating

Convey your armed force of servers with Amazon EC2. In just minutes bring virtual machines-called examples on the web. Select AMI's with operating system of your choice (Linux or Windows) and start deploying your clusters. There are three well known instance types when making EC2 occurrences:

• Compute streamlined. Used for examples that will re🗆uire extremely high re🗆uest rates, this design leverages industry driving processors.

• Memory streamlined. These examples are built with the most efficient per-GB memory cost.

• Storage optimized. Storage optimized EC2 instances access extremely fast SSD storage to serve data retrieval reᐤuests with lightning speed.

For more information about EC2 instances and the different series that can be leveraged against your specific needs, check out the AWS Instance Types page.

Amazon Elastic Compute Cloud (EC2) provides virtual servers - called instances - for figure limit. The EC2 service offers dozens of example types with varying limits and sizes, tailored to specific workload types and applications, such as memory-intensive and accelerated-computing occupations. AWS also gives an Auto Scaling tool to powerfully scale ability to keep up occasion health and performance.

The Amazon EC2 Container Service and EC2 Container Registry enable customers to work with Docker containers and images on the AWS stage. A developer can also use AWS Lambda for serverless functions that automatically run code for applications and services, as well as AWS Elastic Beanstalk for PaaS. AWS also includes Amazon Lightsail, which gives virtual private servers, and AWS Batch, which forms a series of jobs.

Amazon S3: Data stockpiling and development

To build a ground-breaking cloud application you need versatile storage. AWS Simple Storage Services (S3) provides all the required devices to store and move information around the globe utilizing 'buckets.'

AWS S3 simplifies all of your capacity needs into containers called buckets, at that point lets you choose where and how to store them.

There are four ways to designate buckets in AWS and the cost to store them varies greatly.

1) Amazon Standard Storage

For data that are fre🔲uently accessed, such as logs for the last 24 hours or a media file that is being accessed fre🔲uently, Amazon Simple Storage offers reasonable, exceptionally accessible stockpiling capacity that can develop as 🔲uickly as your association needs. You are charged by the gigabyte used and number of demands to access, delete, list, copy or getting an information in S3. Expensive storage arrays are not required to get a new endeavor off the ground.

2) Amazon Infre🔲uent Access Storage

Using the S3 interface, screen and manage resources that are necessary for your operation however are used far less every now and again. By designating these buckets as infre🔲uent get to, information accessibility will be 99.9% (measuring to less than 9 hours of personal time in a year) as compared to 99.99% accessibility (less than a hour of vacation in a year) for standard stockpiling yet can be put away for far less cost per gigabyte than Standard Storage buckets.

3) Amazon Glacier

For profound storage items that must be held however are infrequently used, Amazon Glacier gives long-term filing solutions. Data put away in Glacier can take hours to retrieve instead of seconds, however the cost is a fraction of standard storage. With redundant information destinations all over the world Glacier guarantees your archival data is secure and safe no matter what occurs.

4) Amazon Reduced Redundancy Storage

This service allows for the storing of unimportant, effectively reproducible information, without the same sum of excess and durability as their higher-level capacity tiers.

Understanding these capacity concepts in S3 is essential before building your cloud design. You can learn more about the intricacies of S3 here. Now we should take a look at some of the different AWS administrations that can be utilized to build scalable cloud application.

Amazon Simple Storage Service (S3) provides scalable object storage for data reinforcement, archival and investigation. An IT proficient stores information and records as S3 objects - which can range up to 5 GB - inside S3 buckets to keep them organized. A business can save money with S3 through its Infrequent Access storage level or use Amazon Glacier for long haul cold storage.

Amazon Elastic Block Store gives square level storage volumes for persistent information stockpiling for use with EC2 instances, while Amazon Elastic File System offers oversaw cloud-based file capacity.

A business can likewise relocate data to the cloud by means of storage transport devices, such as AWS Snowball and Snowmobile, or use AWS Storage Gateway to enable on-premises apps to access cloud information.

Databases, information the executives

AWS provides managed database services through its Amazon Relational Database Service, which includes choices for Oracle, SQL Server, PostgreSQL, MySQL, MariaDB and a proprietary high-performance database called Amazon Aurora. AWS offers oversaw NoSQL databases through Amazon DynamoDB.

An AWS client can use Amazon ElastiCache and DynamoDB Accelerator as in-memory data caches for real-time applications. Amazon Redshift offers an information warehouse, which makes it easier for information analysts to perform business knowledge tasks.

Migration, half and half cloud

AWS incorporates various tools and services designed to help clients move applications, databases, servers and information onto its public cloud. The AWS Migration Hub provides a location to screen and oversee migrations from on premises to the cloud. Once in the cloud, EC2 Systems Manager helps an IT team configure on-premises servers and AWS instances.

Amazon also has partnerships with a lot of innovation merchants that ease hybrid cloud deployments. VMware Cloud on AWS brings software-defined data focus innovation from VMware to the AWS cloud. Red Hat Enterprise Linux for Amazon EC2 is the product of another partnership, extending Red Hat's operating system to the AWS cloud.

Systems administration

An Amazon Virtual Private Cloud (VPC) gives an administrator control over a virtual system to use an isolated area of the AWS cloud. AWS consequently provisions new assets within a VPC for extra protection.

Admins can balance system traffic with AWS burden adjusting instruments, including Application Load Balancer and Network Load Balancer. AWS also gives an area name system called Amazon Route 53 that routes end users to applications.

An IT proficient can establish a dedicated connection from an on-premises data center to the AWS cloud via AWS Direct Connect.

Improvement instruments and application administrations

An engineer can take advantage of AWS command-line tools and programming advancement units (SDKs) to deploy and oversee applications and services. The AWS Command Line Interface is Amazon's exclusive code interface. A developer can likewise use AWS Tools for Powershell to manage cloud administrations from Windows environments and AWS Serverless Application Model to simulate an AWS situation to test Lambda capacities. AWS SDKs are available for an assortment of platforms and programming dialects, including Java, PHP, Python, Node.js, Ruby, C++, Android and iOS.

Amazon API Gateway empowers a development team to make, manage and monitor custom APIs that let applications access information or functionality from back-end services. Programming interface Gateway manages a huge number of concurrent API calls at once.

AWS additionally provides a packaged media transcoding administration, Amazon Elastic Transcoder, and a help that imagines workflows for microservices-based applications, AWS Step Functions.

A development team can also make continuous integration and constant conveyance pipelines with services like AWS CodePipeline, AWS CodeBuild, AWS CodeDeploy and AWS CodeStar. An engineer can also store code in Git archives with AWS CodeCommit and evaluate the performance of microservices-based applications with AWS X-Ray.

The board, observing

A admin can oversee and follow cloud resource configuration by means of AWS Config and AWS Config Rules. Those tools, along with AWS Trusted Advisor, can help an IT team avoid inappropriately configured and unnecessarily costly cloud resource deployments.

AWS provides several automation tools in its portfolio. A admin can automate framework provisioning by means of AWS CloudFormation templates, and additionally use AWS OpsWorks and Chef to automate infrastructure and framework configurations.

An AWS customer can monitor resource and application wellbeing with Amazon

CloudWatch and the AWS Personal Health Dashboard, and also use AWS CloudTrail to retain user activity and application programming interface (API) calls for auditing.

Security, administration

AWS gives a range of services for cloud security, including AWS Identity and Access Management (IAM), which permits administrators to define and oversee user access to resources. A admin can also create a client directory with Amazon Cloud Directory, or connect cloud resources to a existing Microsoft Active Directory with the AWS Directory Service. Additionally, AWS Organizations enables a business to establish and manage strategies for various AWS accounts.

The cloud provider has additionally presented instruments that automatically assess potential security risks. Amazon Inspector analyzes an AWS environment for vulnerabilities that may affect security and compliance. Amazon Macie utilizes machine learning technology to secure delicate cloud information.

AWS also includes tools and services that give programming and hardware-based encryption, protect against DDoS attacks, arrangement Secure Sockets Layer and Transport Layer Security certificates and filter possibly harmful traffic to web applications.

Huge information the board, investigation

AWS includes a variety of big data analytics and application services. Amazon Elastic MapReduce offers a Hadoop framework to process large amounts of information, while Amazon Kinesis provides several instruments to process and break down streaming data.

AWS Glue is a service that handles extract, change and load jobs, while the Amazon Elasticsearch Service enables a group to perform application monitoring, log analysis and other tasks with the open source Elasticsearch tool.

To inquiry data, a analyst can use Amazon Athena for S3, and then visualize data with Amazon QuickSight.

Man-made brainpower

AWS offers a scope of AI model advancement and conveyance platforms, as well as bundled AI-based applications. The Amazon AI suite of tools incorporates Amazon Lex for voice and text chatbot technology, Amazon Polly for content to-discourse translation and Amazon Rekognition for image and facial investigation. AWS also provides technology for engineers to build keen apps that rely on machine learning innovation and complex algorithms.

With AWS Deep Learning AMIs, developers can create and train custom AI models with clusters of GPUs or compute-optimized occasions. AWS likewise includes profound learning development structures for MXNet and TensorFlow.

On the consumer side, AWS technologies power the Alexa Voice Services, and a developer can use the Alexa Skills Kit to build voice-based apps for Echo gadgets.

Portable improvement

The AWS Mobile Hub offers a collection of tools and administrations for portable application developers, including the AWS Mobile SDK, which provides code tests and libraries.

A portable application developer can additionally use Amazon Cognito to manage client access to mobile applications, as well as Amazon Pinpoint to send push notices to application end users and then analyze the effectiveness of those communications.

Messages, notices

AWS messaging services give center communication for users and applications. Amazon Simple Queue Service is an overseen message ⊠ueue that sends, stores and receives messages between components of distributed applications to ensure that the parts of an application work as intended.

Amazon Simple Notification Service (SNS) enables a business to send pub-sub messages to endpoints, such as end clients or administrations. SNS incorporates a portable messaging feature that empowers push messaging to mobile gadgets. Amazon Simple Email Service provides a stage for IT experts and marketers to send and get emails.

Versatile Load Balancing: Scalable execution

Amazon incorporates a powerful, versatile load balancing solution in AWS Elastic Load Balancer (ELB). ELB ensures that client requests are sent to the appropriate servers and avoiding any server hotspots (over-utilizing one server and under utilizing others)

AWS supports two types of burden adjusting: classic Load adjusting and Application Load Balancing.

• Classic Load Balancing, which analyzes basic network and application information and guarantee fault tolerance if one of the EC2 instances running web application happens to fail.

• Application Load Balancing, which looks at content request and routes traffic to the appropriate container or microservice based on the Application content data.

As with most AWS services, you only pay for the administrations that you use. If there should be an occurrence of ELB service, you pay for by an hour and by the sum of data processed.

CloudFront: Deliver a superior client experience

Amazon Cloudfront is a global content delivery system that leverages Amazon's vast global infrastructure to deliver contents with optimized speed and cost. CloudFront guarantees that content is closer to the users and improves the client experience by conveying the content quicker by serving the content from the AWS region closer to the end user.

Cloudfront works consistently with AWS services. With no least usage commitment, experimenting with configurations and instances to find ways to improve execution is extremely simple.

Flexible Block Store (EBS): Low-latency instance get to

AWS Elastic Block Storage provides persistent Block-level storage volumes for your EC2 occurrences with low dormancy. It also permits your system to get to high speed SSD stockpiling and layer your security with Access Control Lists and encryption.

Amazon Route 53: The AWS DNS service

Handle DNS routing with the high-speed, low cost Route 53 help from AWS. Translate machine hosts and named application to IP addresses and back inside your VPC and connect resources like web servers, S3 containers, and elastic load balancers. Route 53 is the arrange of DNS Servers hosted in various AWS regions all around the world. Utilizing API, engineers can easily automate the setup changes to Route 53.

Cloudwatch: Monitor your AWS condition

Cloudwatch is the local monitoring service for assets and applications running in AWS. Gather logs and monitor measurements for key resources like:

- Amazon EC2 instance

- Amazon DynamoDB tables

- Amazon RDS DB instances

- Custom measurements generated by your applications and administrations

With Cloudwatch you can accomplish full perceivability into all of your AWS components.

Optional AWS Support Services

In addition to the essential cloud administrations, Amazon offers a host of optional products for enhancing and securing your cloud ecosystem. Here's a look at some of the more popular helper services.

The nearly limitless possibilities of AWS are wrangled down into manageable control screens, showing you how all of your virtual apparatuses are meshing together.

Lambda: Functions for optimized compute

Pay only for the actual milliseconds of figure time your code re🔲uire to execute and avoid complexity and management overhead of configuring and managing underlying AWS infrastructure. AWS Lambda abstracts fundamental AWS infrastructure and allows engineers to center around running their code.

AWS Config: Infrastructure management

Keep a bird's eye see on your AWS infrastructure and stay secure and agreeable with AWS Config. See up to date asset stock and track any changes to your infrastructure from one helpful administration board.

Elastic Beanstalk: Build and scale incredible web applications

As the name infers, it's outlandish to grow quicker than Elastic Beanstalk, the AWS apparatus for deploying and managing web applications designed in most of the top programming dialects. The adjustable autoscale settings allow your apps to develop and contract as needed to avoid latency and wasted asset utilization.

CloudTrail: Monitor and audit activity

Application program interfaces calls (APIs) take place within your condition at a rate that can vary from a couple transactions per minute to millions per second. AWS Cloudtrail captures key information about these transactions, including the source IP address, the event time, and more. The data from CloudTrail is especially basic for meeting security standards and complying with internal audits and standards or regulations, for example, PCI and HIPAA.

Amazon EFS: Manage your documents

Rapidly and easily create document systems through a simple web interface with Amazon Elastic File System (EFS). EFS develops and shrinks your file storage system as required so you never run out of space. Mount one file system to multiple

EC2 occurrences to share regular information and outstanding burden sources, oversee access control records, and more with EFS.

These services add monstrous adaptability, scalability, and observing highlights that will help your association ace your VPC condition in AWS.

Unique Purpose AWS Apps

Amazon also offers some highly specialized apparatuses for getting the most out of your cloud resources. Amazon's comprehensive list of items and administrations is far reaching, yet these are some of the most popular specialty apps.

Kinesis: Optimize data stream

A three-pronged tool for fine tuning multimedia data stream, Amazon Kinesis is a stage for loading and analyzing streaming information. It consists of:

Kinesis Firehose, a gushing analytics service, which ingests up to terabytes of information and send it to different AWS administrations such as S3, Redshift and AWS ES.

Kinesis Analytics, which lets you gather masses of data via straightforward SQL inquiries, with no need to bring in developers versed in complex programming languages.

Kinesis Streams, which takes these torrents of data and intuitively helps you create custom applications for preparing it. With Kinesis Streams you can:

Elastically scale your environment to respond to volume.

Change terabytes of raw streaming information into intuitive dashboards.

Generate cautions when basic events take place.

Trigger computerized responses to common problems like inertness.

Coordinate with other Kinesis elements and AWS to optimize delivery.

VPC Flow: Analyze your traffic

VPC flow logs are detailed records of the IP traffic passing to and from a lone port, a subnet, or your entire VPC environment. Flow logs enable you to get into the deep investigation subtleties about who is going where and when. The data they provide about your system will help you create architecture and budget plans for progressing activities and also allows you to conduct network forensics using the VPC flow logs—including what traffic is worth the compute and storage cost of capturing.

DynamoDB: Fast, simple database get to

Amazon DynamoDB is a completely managed NoSQL database service in AWS. It works with document and key-value storage models, and its high accessibility and flexibility make it perfect for gaming, mobile applications, and more. Spin up databases with ease and spare on compute expenses with DynamoDB.

There is much more to the AWS universe than a short guide can detail. Be that as it may, familiarity with the above fundamentals sets you up to expand your organization's framework to the cloud, build a entirely new condition, and ace the art of data logging to guarantee compliance and security. You can learn more about AWS in the video beneath, read up on AWS logging best practices, check out the Sumo Logic App for AWS, or pursue a free trial.

Other services

Amazon Web Services has a range of business productivity SaaS options. The Amazon Chime service empowers online video gatherings, calls and text-based chats across gadgets. A business can additionally take favorable position of Amazon

WorkDocs, a document stockpiling and sharing service, and Amazon WorkMail, a business email administration with calendaring features.

Work area and spilling application services incorporate Amazon WorkSpaces, a remote desktop-as-a-service platform, and Amazon AppStream, a service that lets a developer stream a desktop application from AWS to a end user's web browser.

AWS also has a variety of services that enable internet of things (IoT) arrangements. The AWS IoT service provides a back-end platform to manage IoT devices and data ingestion to other AWS stockpiling and database services. The AWS IoT Button provides hardware for restricted IoT functionality, and AWS Greengrass brings AWS compute abilities to IoT gadgets.

AWS evaluating models and competition

AWS offers a compensation as-you-go model for its cloud services, either on a per-hour or per-second basis. There is also a choice to reserve a set amount of compute capacity at a discounted price for clients who prepay in entire, or who sign up for one-or three-year use responsibilities.

AMAZON WEB SEVICES - AN OVERVIEW

You might be pardoned if you're perplexed about how Amazon, which started out as an online bookstore, has become the leading cloud registering provider. This chapter solves that secret by discussing the circumstances that led Amazon into the cloud figuring services field and why Amazon Web Services, far from being an oddly different offering from a retailer, is a logical outgrowth of Amazon's business.

A section of this book also compares Amazon's cloud offering to other competitors in the market and clarifies how its methodology varies. As part of this comparison, I present some statistics on the size and growth of Amazon's offering, while describing why it's difficult to get a handle on its exact size.

Another part closes with a brief discourse about the Amazon Web Services biological system and why it is far more extravagant than what Amazon itself provides — and why it offers more value for clients of Amazon's cloud service.

Be that as it may, before I uncover all the answers to the Amazon mystery, I answer an even more fundamental question: What is all this cloud computing stuff, anyway?

ELABORATING CLOUD COMPUTING

I believe that skill is built on a foundation of knowledge. Anyone who wants to work with Amazon Web Services (AWS, starting now and into the foreseeable future) ought to have a firm understanding of distributed computing — what it is and what it gives. IaaS, Paas, SaaS As a general overview, cloud computing refers to the delivery of computing services from a remote location over a network. The National Institute of Standards and Technology (NIST), a U.S. government agency, has a definition of cloud computing that is by and large considered the gold standard. Rather than trying to make my possess definition, I always defer to NIST's definition. The following information is drawn directly from it.

Cloud computing is a model for enabling pervasive, convenient, ondemand network access to a shared pool of configurable computing resources (e.g., systems, servers, storage, applications, and services) that can be rapidly provisioned and released with minimal management effort or service provider interaction.

This cloud model is made out of five basic characteristics:

✓ **On-demand self-service:** A consumer can singularly arrangement computing capabilities, such as server time and network capacity, automatically as required without reuiring human connection with each service provider.

✓ **Broad network access:** Capabilities are available over the network and accessed through standard systems that promote use by heterogeneous slight or thick client stages, (for example, mobile phones, tablets, workstations, and workstations).

✓ **Resource pooling:** The provider's computing resources are pooled to serve multiple purchasers using a multi-tenant model, with different physical and virtual assets dynamically assigned and reassigned according to shopper request. There's a sense of alleged location independence, in that the customer generally has no control or knowledge over the exact location of the provided assets yet may be able to determine area at a higher level of abstraction (by country, state, or data center, for example). Models of resources are storage, processing, memory, and network bandwidth.

✓ **Rapid versatility:** Capabilities can be elastically provisioned and released, in some cases automatically, to scale rapidly outward and internal commensurate with demand. To the consumer, the capabilities available for provisioning often appear to be unlimited and can be appropriated in any Ⓠuantity at any time.

✓ **Measured help:** Cloud systems automatically control and optimize asset use by leveraging a metering capability at a level of deliberation that's suitable to the type of service (stockpiling, handling, transmission capacity, or active user accounts, for model). Resource usage can be monitored, controlled, and reported, providing straightforwardness for both the supplier and consumer of the utilized administration.

Cloud computing is commonly described as providing three types of functionality, alluded to IaaS, PaaS, and SaaS, where aaS is shorthand for "as a service" and service implies that the functionality isn't local to the client yet rather originates elsewhere (a area in a remote location accessed via a network). The letters I, P, and S in the acronyms allude to distinctive types of functionality, as the following list makes clear:

✓ **Infrastructure as a Service (Iaas):** Offers users the basic building blocks of computing: processing, network connectivity, and storage. (Of course, you also need other capabilities in order to fully support IaaS functionality — such as client accounts, usage tracking, and security.) You would use an IaaS cloud provider if you need to build a application from scratch and need get to to fairly low-level functionality within the operating system.

√ **Platform as a Service (PaaS):** Instead of offering low-level capacities within the operating system, offers more significant level programming frameworks that a developer interacts with to obtain computing services. For example, rather than open a file and write a collection of bits to it, in a PaaS situation the developer just calls a capacity and then provides the function with the collection of bits. The PaaS framework then handles the snort work, such as opening a file, writing the bits to it, and ensuring that the bits have been successfully received by the document system. The PaaS framework supplier takes care of sponsorship up the information and overseeing the collection of reinforcements, for example, thus relieving the user of having to complete further troublesome administrative tasks.

✓ **Software as a Service (SaaS):** Has climbed to an even higher rung on the transformative ladder than PaaS. With SaaS, all application functionality is conveyed over a system in a pretty bundle. The client need do nothing more than utilize the application; the SaaS provider deals with the issue associated with making and working the application, segregating client information, providing security for each user as well as the overall SaaS environment, and taking care of a myriad of other details.

As with every model, this division into I, P, and S provides a certain informative leverage and looks for to make neat and clean an element that in real life can be rather convoluted. In the case of IPS, the model is presented as though the types are cleanly defined though they no longer are. Many cloud providers offer administrations of more than one type. Amazon, specifically, has begun to provide many platform-like services as it has built out its contributions, and has even ventured into a few out and out application administrations that you'd associate with SaaS. You could state that Amazon provides all three types of cloud computing.

Cloud Computing (Private-versus-public)

On the off chance that you find the mix of I, P, and S in the former section confusing, wait 'til you hear about the whole private-versus-public cloud computing distinction.

Note the seＺuence of events:

1. Amazon, as the first cloud computing provider, offers public cloud computing — anyone can use it.

2. Many IT organizations, when examining this new Amazon Web Services creature, asked why they couldn't create and offer an assistance like AWS to their possess users, hosted in their own data focuses. This on premise version became known as private cloud computing.

3. Proceeding the pattern, several facilitating providers thought they could offer their IT customers an isolated part of their information centers and let customers build mists there. This idea can likewise be considered private cloud figuring because it's dedicated to one client. On the other hand, because the data to and from this private cloud runs over a shared network, is the cloud truly private?

4. At last, after one brilliant bulb noted that companies may not pick only public or private, the term hybrid was derived in order to offer companies that are making use of public as well aa private cloud environments.

Amazon Business Philosophy – Having A Full Understanding

Amazon Web Services was officially uncovered to the world on March 13, 2006. On that day, AWS offered the Simple Storage Service, its first service. (As you may envision, Simple Storage Services was before long abbreviated to S3.) The thought behind S3 was simple: It could offer the idea of article storage over the web, a setup where anybody could put an item — essentially, any bunch of bytes — into S3.

Those bytes may contain a digital photograph or a document reinforcement or a product package or a video or audio recording or a spreadsheet record or — well, you get the thought.

S3 was relatively limited when it first began out. Though items could, admittedly, be written or read from anywhere, they could be stored in only one region: the United States. Moreover, objects could be no larger than 5 gigabytes — not tiny by any methods, however certainly smaller than many documents that people may need to store in S3. The actions accessible for objects were also ⬚uite restricted: You could write, read, and delete them, and that was it.

In its first six years, S3 has grown in all dimensions. The service is presently offered throughout the world in various areas. Objects can now be as large as 5 terabytes. S3 can also offer many more capabilities regarding objects. A object would now be able to have an end date, for model: You can set a date and time after which a object is no longer accessible for access. (This capability may be valuable if you want to make a video available for viewing for only a certain period, such as the next about fourteen days.) S3 can now also be used to host websites — in other words, individual pages can be put away as objects, and your domain name (say, www.example.com) can point to S3, which serves up the pages.

S3 did not remain the solitary AWS example for long. Just a few months after it was launched, Amazon began offering Simple Queue Service (SQS), which provides an approach to pass messages between different programs. SQS can accept or deliver messages within the AWS environment or outside the environment to other programs (your web program, for example) and can be used to fabricate exceptionally versatile conveyed applications.

Later in 2006 came Elastic Compute Cloud (known tenderly as EC2). As the AWS computing service, EC2 offers computing capacity on demand, with quick accessibility and no set commitment to length of use. Don't stress if this depiction of AWS seems overpowering at first — in the rest of this book, you can find out about the different pieces of AWS, how they work, and how you can use them to address your registering necessities.

This section gives a system in which to comprehend the genesis of AWS, with details to pursue. The significant thing for you to understand is the manner by which AWS got started, how big of a change it represents in the way figuring is done, and why it's significant to your future. The overall pattern of AWS has been to add additional administrations steadily, and afterward rapidly improve each service over time. AWS is now made out of more than 25 different services, many offered with different abilities via diverse configurations or formats. This rich set of services can be mixed and matched to create interesting and interesting applications, limited only by your creative mind or needs.

So, from one simple service (S3) to more than 25 in just over six years, and throughout the world — and developing and improving all the time! You're presumably impressed by how quick all of this has happened. You're not alone. Within the industry, Amazon is regarded with a mixture of awe and envy because of how quickly it conveys new AWS functionality. On the off chance that you're intrigued, you can keep up with changes to AWS via its What's New web page on the AWS site, at http://aws.amazon.com/about-aws/whats-new

This torrid pace of improvement is great news for you because it means that AWS constantly presents new things you can do — things you probably couldn't do in the past on the grounds that the AWS functionality would be too troublesome to implement or too costly to afford even if you could actualize it.

Estimating the size of AWS

Amazon is the pioneer of cloud processing and, on the grounds that you'd have to have been living under a rock not to have heard about "the cloud," being the pioneer in this area is a big deal. The obvious question is this: If AWS is the big dog in the advertise and if cloud computing is the most sweltering thing since cut bread, how big are we talking about?

That is an intriguing inquiry since Amazon uncovers little about the degree of its business. Rather than break out AWS revenues, the company lumps them into an Other category in its financial reports.

By the by, we have some pieces of information to its size, based on information from the company itself and on informed hypothesis by industry pundits.

Amazon itself provides a proxy for the growth of the AWS service. Every so often, it announces how many objects are stored in the S3 service. Given that pace of growth, it's obvious that the matter of AWS is blasting. Other estimates of the size of the AWS service exist too. A very clever specialist named Huan Liu examined AWS IP addresses and anticipated the total number of server racks held by AWS, in view of an gauge of how numerous servers reside in a rack.

In the event that you consider that each server can bolster a number of virtual machines (the number would shift, obviously, according to the size of the virtual machines), AWS could support several million running virtual machines. Amazon publishes a list of open IP addresses; as of May 2013, there are more than 4,000,000 accessible in AWS. This number is not inconsistent with Liu's estimated number of physical servers; it's also an advantageous place to look to track how much AWS is growing.

Checking the reality

Though Amazon doesn't announce how many dollars AWS pulls in, that hasn't halted others from making their own estimates of the size of AWS business — and their gauges make it clear that AWS is a very large business indeed.

Early in 2012, several experts from Morgan Stanley broke down the AWS business and made a decision about that the service pulled in $1.19 billion in 2011. (You gotta love the accuracy that these pundits come up with, eh?) Other analysts from JP Morgan Chase and UBS have determined that AWS will achieve 2015 revenues of around $2.5 billion.

The bottom line: AWS is big and getting bigger (and better) every day. It truly is no embellishment to state that AWS speaks to an upheaval in registering. Individuals are doing amazing things with it, and this book shows you how you can take advantage of it.

The AWS Infrastructure

In the event that what Amazon is doing with AWS represents an upheaval, as I depict in the previous section, how is the company bringing it about? In other words, how is it conveying this amazing service? Throughout this book, I go into the points of interest of how the service operates, however until further notice I diagram the general methodology that Amazon has taken in structure AWS.

First and foremost, Amazon has approached the work in a special design, befitting a company that changed the face of retail. Amazon specializes in a low-edge approach to business, and it carries that perspective into AWS. Unlike almost every other player in the cloud computing market, Amazon has focused on creating a low-edge, profoundly efficient offering, and that offering starts with the way Amazon has built out its foundation.

Making hard equipment choices

Not at all like most of its rivals, Amazon builds its hardware infrastructure from product components. Commodity, in this case, alludes to using equipment from lesser-known manufacturers who charge less than their brand name contenders. For components for which commodity offerings aren't available, Amazon (known as a ferocious negotiator) gets absolute bottom prices.

On the hardware side of the AWS offering, Amazon's approach is clear: Buy equipment as cheaply as conceivable. In any case, wait, you may state, won't the commodity approach result in a less dependable infrastructure? After all, the brand-name hardware providers attest that one benefit of paying premium costs is that you get higher-quality gear. Well . . . yes and no. It may be genuine that premiumpriced equipment (traditionally called enterprise equipment because of the assumption that large ventures require more reliability and are willing to pay extra to obtain it) is more dependable in an apples-to-apples examination. That is, a enterprise-grade server keeps going longer and endures less outages than its product class partner.

The issue, from Amazon's perspective, is how much more reliable the venture gear is than the commodity version, and how much that improved reliability is worth. In other words, it needs to know the money saving advantage ratio of enterprise-versus-commodity.

Making this evaluation more challenging is a fundamental reality: At the scale on which an Amazon works (remember that it has nearly a large portion of a million servers running in its AWS service), e?uipment — no matter who provides it — is breaking all the time.

In the event that you're a cloud provider with an foundation the size of Amazon's, you have to accept, for each type of equipment you use, a endless round of crashed disk drives, fried motherboards, packet-dropping organize switches, and on and on.

Therefore, even if you purchase the highest-?uality, most expensive gear available, you'll still end up (if you're blessed enough to grow into a very huge cloud computing provider like, say, Amazon) with an unreliable foundation. Put another way, at a huge scale, even highly reliable individual components still result in an unreliable overall infrastructure because of the disappointment of components, as uncommon as the failure of a specific piece of e?uipment may be.

The scale at which Amazon operates influences different perspectives of its hardware framework as well. Other than components, for example, servers, networks, and storage, data centers also have control supplies, cooling, generators, and backup batteries. Depending on the specific component, Amazon may have to use custom-designed hardware to work at the scale re?uired.

Think of AWS hardware infrastructure this way: If you had to design and operate server farms to manage massive scale and in a way that aligns with a corporate order to operate inexpensively, you'd probably end up with a solution much like Amazon's. You'd use commodity computing gear whenever possible, jawbone prices down when you couldn't obtain item contributions, and custom-design e▯uipment to manage your unusually largescale operation.

Looking at Amazon's software infrastructure strategy

Because of Amazon's low-edge, highly scaled necessities, you'd most likely expect it to have an uni▯ue approach to the cloud computing programming infrastructure running on top of its hardware environment, right?

You'd be right.

Amazon has created a one of a kind, exceptionally specialized programming environment in order to provide its cloud computing services. I stress the word unique because, at first glance, individuals regularly discover AWS different and befuddling — it is not at all like any other computing condition they've already encountered. After users see how AWS operates, however, they for the most part find that its design makes sense and that it's appropriate for what it delivers — and, more important, for how people use the service.

Though Amazon has an unusual approach to its hardware condition, it's in the programming infrastructure that its uniqueness truly stands out. Give me a chance to give you a speedy outline of its highlights. The software foundation is

✓ Based on virtualization: Virtualization — an innovation that digests software components from reliance on their underlying equipment — lies at the heart of AWS. Being ready to create virtual machines, start them, end them, and restart them ⬚uickly makes the AWS service conceivable.

As you may expect, Amazon has drawn closer virtualization in an uni⬚ue fashion. Normally, it wanted a minimal effort way to use virtualization, so it chose the open source Xen Hypervisor as its software establishment. Then it made significant changes to the "vanilla" Xen product so that it could fulfill the re?uirements of AWS.

The result is that Amazon leverages virtualization, yet the virtualization arrangement it came up with is stretched out in manners that help vast scale and a plethora of administrations worked on it.

✓ **Operated as a service:** I know what you're going to say: "Of course it's worked as an assistance — that is the reason it's called Amazon Web Services!" That's true, however Amazon needed to make a huge software framework in request to be able to offer its processing capability as a service.

For example, Amazon had to create a way for users to operate their AWS assets from a distance and with no prerequisite for neighborhood hands-on cooperation. What's more, it had to segregate a client's assets from everyone else's assets in a way that ensures security, in light of the fact that nobody wants other users to be able to see, access, or change his assets.

Amazon had to provide a set of interfaces — an Application Programming Interface (API) — to permit users to manage each aspect of AWS.

✓ **Designed for flexibility:** Amazon designed AWS to address users like itself — users that need rich computing administrations available at a minute's notice to support their application needs and constantly changing business conditions.

In other words, just as Amazon can't predict what its computing requirements will be in a year or two, neither can the advertise for which Amazon fabricated AWS.

In that situation, it bodes well to implement few limitations on the administration. Thusly, instead of offer a tightly integrated set of services that provides just a few ways to use them, Amazon provides a highly granular set of services that can be "mixed and coordinated" by the user to create a application that meets its exact needs.

By designing the administration in a highly adaptable fashion, Amazon enables its customers to be innovative, thereby supporting innovation. All through the book, I'll offer examples of some of the interesting things organizations are doing with AWS.

Not only are the computing administrations themselves highly adaptable, the conditions of use of AWS are flexible as well. You need nothing more to get started than a e-mail address and a credit card.

✓ **Highly versatile:** If you took the message from prior in the section about the intrinsic lack of quality of hardware to heart, you now perceive that there is no way to implement resiliency via equipment. The conspicuous alternative is with programming, and that is the path Amazon has chosen. Amazon makes AWS highly resilient by implementing resource redundancy — essentially using multiple copies of a resource to ensure that disappointment of a single resource does not cause the service to fail. For example, if you were to store just one copy of each of your objects within its S3 service, that object may sometimes be inaccessible on the grounds that the disk drive on which it resides has broken down. Instead, AWS keeps multiple copies of an object, guaranteeing that even if one – or two! – objects become unavailable due to hardware disappointment, users can still access the item, subsequently improving S3 reliability and strength.

In rundown, Amazon has actualized a rich software infrastructure to allow clients get to to large ⬛uantities of processing resources at absolute bottom prices.

The AWS Ecosystem

Thus far, I haven't delved too profoundly into the different pieces of the AWS puzzle, yet it ought to be clear (if you're reading this chapter from start to finish) that Amazon offers a number of services to its users.

However, AWS has a far more extravagant set of services than only the ones it gives. In fact, users can find nearly everything they need within the limits of AWS to make almost any application they may want to execute. These services are available via the AWS ecosystem – the contributions of Amazon partners and outsiders that host their contributions on AWS.

In this way, moreover to the 25+ administrations AWS itself offers, users can find administrations that

✓ Offer preconfigured virtual machines with software components as of now installed and arranged, to enable ⬚uick use

✓ Manipulate pictures

✓ Transmit or stream video

✓ Integrate applications with one another

✓ Monitor application performance

✓ Ensure application security

✓ Operate billing and subscriptions

✓ Manage medicinal services claims

✓ Offer real bequest for deal

✓ Analyze genomic information

✓ Host websites

✓ Provide client assistance

Furthermore, really, this list scarcely scratches the surface of what's accessible inside AWS. As it were, AWS is a current bazaar, providing an unbelievably rich set of computing abilities from anyone who decides to set up shop to anybody who decides to purchase what's being offered.

On closer inspection, you can see that the AWS environment is made up of three distinct subsystems:

✓ AWS registering services provided by Amazon: As noted prior, Amazon currently provides more than 25 AWS services and is launching more all the time. AWS provides a large range of cloud processing services — you'll be introduced to many of them over the course of this book.

✓ Computing administrations provided by third parties that operate on AWS: These administrations tend to offer functionality that enables you to assemble applications of a type that AWS doesn't strictly offer. For example, AWS offers some billing capability to empower clients to build applications and charge individuals to utilize them, however the AWS service doesn't support many charging use cases — user-specific discounts based on the size of the company, for example. Many companies (and even individuals) offer administrations integral to AWS that then allow clients to build richer applications more ✷uickly.

✓ Complete applications offered by third parties that keep running on AWS: You can use these services, regularly alluded to as SaaS (Software as a Service), over a network without having to install them on your own hardware. Many, many organizations host their applications on AWS, drawn to it for the same reasons that end clients are drawn to it: low cost, simple access, and high scalability. A interesting pattern within

AWS is the expanding move by traditional software merchants to migrate their applications to AWS and provide them as SaaS offerings rather than as applications that users install from a CD or DVD on their own machines.

As you go forward with using AWS, be careful to recognize the differences between these three offerings inside the AWS ecosystem, especially Amazon's role (or lack thereof) in all three. Though outsider services or SaaS applications can be extraordinarily valuable to your computing endeavors, Amazon, quite sensibly, offers no support or ensure about their usefulness or performance.

It's up to you to choose whether a given non-AWS service is fit for your needs. Amazon, continually working to make it ever easier to locate and incorporate third party services into your application, has created the Amazon Marketplace as your go-to place for finding AWS-empowered applications. Moreover, being part of the Marketplace suggests an underwriting by AWS, which will make you progressively sure about using a Marketplace application.

Counting Up the Network Effects Benefit

The reason the AWS biological system has become the processing commercial center for all and sundry can be caught in the expression network effect, which can be thought of as the value derived from a network because other system participants are part of the network. The classic case of a network effect is the phone: The more people who use telephones, the more value

there is to someone getting a telephone —
on the grounds that the larger the number of
telephones being used, the easier it is to
communicate with a large number of
individuals.

Conversely, if you're the only person in
town with a phone, well, you're going to be
truly desolate — and not very chatty! Said
another way, for a service with network
impacts, the more people who use it, the
more attractive it is to potential users, and
the more value they receive when they use
the service.

From the AWS point of view, the network
impact means that, in case you're giving a
new cloud-based service, it makes sense to
offer it where lots of other cloud clients are
found — someplace like AWS, for instance.
This system impact benefits AWS

extraordinarily, simply because numerous individuals, when they start to think about doing something with cloud computing, naturally gravitate to AWS in light of the fact that it's an image name that they recognize.

In any case, concerning AWS, there's a even greater arrange effect than the fact that lots of people are using it: The technical aspects of AWS have an impact as well.

When one administration talks to another over the Internet, a certain sum of time passes when the correspondence between the services ventures over the Internet arrange — even at the speed of light, information voyaging long distances takes a certain sum of time. Also, while data is bridging the Internet, it's continually being shunted through routers to guarantee that it's being sent in the right bearing. This combination of organize length and gadget interaction is called inactivity, a measure of how much of a delay is imposed by network traffic separation.

In concrete terms, if you use a web browser to access data from a website hosted inside 50 miles of you, it will likely react quicker than if the same site were facilitated 7,000 miles away. To proceed this concept, using a service that is found nearby makes your application run faster — always a decent thing. So if your service runs on AWS, you'd like any administrations you rely upon to also run on AWS — because the latency influencing your application is much lower than if those services began some place else.

People who build services tend to be smart, so they'll notice that their potential clients like the thought of having services nearby. In the event that you're setting up a new service, you'll be pulled in to AWS because parts of other services are already located there. Furthermore, if you're considering utilizing a cloud service, you're likely to pick AWS because the number of administrations there will make it simpler to build your application, from the perspective of service accessibility and low latency performance.

The network effects associated with AWS give you a rich set of administrations to influence as you create applications to run on Amazon's cloud offering. They can work to reduce your outstanding burden and speed your application development conveyance by relieving you of much of the trouble generally associated with integrating external programming components and services into your application.

Here are some benefits of being capable to influence the network effects of the AWS ecosystem in your application:

✓ The administration is as of now up and running inside AWS. You don't have to obtain the software, install it, design it, test it, and then integrate it into your application. Because it's already operational in the AWS environment, you can skip straightforwardly to the last step — perform the specialized mix.

✓ The administrations have a cloud-friendly licensing model. Vendors have already figured out how to offer their programming and charge for it in the AWS condition. Vendors often align with the AWS charging methodology, charging per hour of use or offering a subscription for monthly access. In any case, one thing you don't have to do is approach a merchant that has a large, upfront permit fee and arrange to operate in the AWS environment — it's already taken care of.

✓ Support is accessible for the service. You don't need to figure out why a software component you want to use doesn't work properly in the AWS environment — the vendor takes responsibility for it. In the parlance of the world of help, you have, as the technology industry rather indelicately puts it, a throat to gag.

✓ Performance improves. Because the administration works in the same condition that your application runs in, it provides low inactivity and helps your application perform better.

Before you start thinking about finding a packaged programming application to incorporate into your application, or about writing your own programming segment to give certain functionality, search the Marketplace to see whether at least one applications already give the fundamental usefulness.

AWS versus Other Cloud Providers

Nature abhors a vacuum, and markets abhor monopoly suppliers, so it stands to reason that competitors always enter an attractive showcase. Distributed computing is no different: There are a plethora of distributed computing suppliers. Normally, you'll want to get the lowdown on how AWS measures up. The most significant contrast between AWS and almost all other cloud suppliers revolves around what showcase they target. To understand that aspect, you must understand the premise of the service they offer. Now, AWS grew out of the abilities that Amazon created to enable its developers to rapidly create and deploy applications. The administration is focused on making developers more productive and, in a word, more joyful.

By contrast, most other cloud providers have a facilitating heritage: Their experiences include supporting infrastructure for IT operations groups responsible for maintaining framework uptime. A critical part of the value suggestion for hosting suppliers has generally been the high ꤰuality of their infrastructures — in other words, the undertaking idea of their servers, systems, stockpiling, and so on.

This legacy carries several implications about big business cloud suppliers:

✓ The focus is on the concerns of IT operations rather than on the worries of engineers. Regularly, this concern translates as, "The administration isn't easy to use." For example, an enterprise cloud provider may require a discussion with a sales representative before granting access to the administration and then force a back-and-forth manual process as part of the account setup. By contrast, AWS permits anyone with an email address and a charge card access to the service within ten minutes.

✓ The service itself reflects its hosting legacy, with its usefulness and use model reflecting how physical servers operate. Often, the only storage a enterprise cloud service provider offers is related with individual virtual machines — no object storage, such as S3, is offered, in light of the fact that it isn't part of a typical hosting environment.

✓ Enterprise cloud service suppliers often re❓uire a multiyear commitment to asset use with a particular level of computing limit. Though this system makes it simpler for a cloud specialist co-op to plan its business, it's much less convenient for clients — and it imposes some of the same issues that they're trying to escape from!

✓ The use of enterprise e❓uipment often implies higher costs when analyzed to AWS. I have seen undertaking cloud service suppliers charge 800 percent more than

AWS. Depending on organization re◻uirements and the idea of the application, clients may be willing to pay a premium for these providers; on the other hand, higher prices and the long haul commitment that often goes with the utilization of an AWS contender may strike many users as unattractive or even unacceptable.

The rise of shadow IT

Disappointment at being unable to get hold of server resources in a timely style has led to the wonder of shadow IT: developers bypassing IT appropriate and obtaining resources themselves.

This phenomenon is powerful and growing — at one conference, I heard a CIO state that he had examined the cost reports submitted to him for repayment and found more than 50 different AWS accounts being utilized by his improvement staff!

Here's something to consider: Shadow IT is a pejorative term, implying stealth and a distinct whiff of unlawful conduct. On the other hand, somebody engaging in shadow IT might, reasonably enough, think of it as "getting the job done" in the face of existing processes that can stretch out to several months the length of time required to obtain assets.

This strife is unlikely to subside in the close future. Developers relish the freedom and adaptability that AWS provides, though many IT groups are engaged in a fruitless struggle to go back to "the great old days," where they set the rules.

The conflict will ultimately be resolved in support of designers. The reason is straightforward: The application is the way businesses gain esteem from IT, and applications are often directly tied to revenue-generating offerings (state, a portable phone app that empowers users to request goods or services online). Infrastructure, the territory of standard IT, is then seen as a necessary evil — the pipes that supports applications.

The preferred position held by developers can be seen in cloud computing market share. One technology expert told me that, by his estimate, AWS represents 75 percent of the market for cloud administration providers. I anticipate that weight should build on enterprise cloud suppliers to rapidly improve their offerings to include more designer friendly administrations. Amazon's six-year head start may make it too elusive to surpass.

In the event that you analyze how well Amazon matches up against the NIST definition of cloud computing (discussed at the beginning if this chapter) when compared with its competitors, AWS more often than not emerges victorious. In part, that's because AWS was the pioneer, and because the first entrant into a market typically gets to define it. There's more to it than that, though.

Amazon's stroke of virtuoso was to put together a innovative offering tending to a market inadequately served by traditional IT practices. In spite of the fact that hosting organizations typically serve IT operations groups well, the emphasis on enterprise hardware and high uptime availability frustrates developers trying to get access to resources. Stories of waiting weeks or months for servers to be provisioned are overflowing within the industry. As you may envision, developers (and the application managers and executives they work for) ached for a different way of doing things — and that's what AWS offers.

Getting Ready for the 21st Century

This chapter gives an review of Amazon Web Services. It lets you perceive how AWS has developed from Amazon's own processing needs and infrastructure to now represent Amazon's reaction to this basic hypothesis: If we need a flexible, cost-effective, and profoundly scalable infrastructure, a lot of other organizations could probably use one as well."

From that initial understanding, Amazon made the processing stage of the 21st century. Directed at developers, and gave all through the world, AWS is experiencing explosive development as more and more individuals explore how it can empower them to settle problems that were unsolvable by the conventional methods of managing infrastructure.

I hope that you can't wait to bounce in to investigating AWS. This book aims to furnish you with knowledge you need so that you, too, can leverage the amazing AWS distributed computing offering.

AWS Management Console

Alright, so you are ready to start working with Amazon Web Services (AWS) alongside cloud computing. However, how? Well, it turns out that the services part of Amazon Web Services refers to the fact that all interaction with Amazon's distributed computing administration is performed with the help of numerous Application Programming Interface (API) calls over the Internet. These calls are accomplished by either SOAP or REST interfaces conveying data in XML or JSON formats.

Whew! Sounds confounded.

Never dread. Amazon offers its own, web-based interface to empower users to work with AWS. This interface, the AWS Management Console, hides all the complex details of interacting with the AWS API. You interact with the comfort, and Amazon's program deals with all the unpredictability under the hood. In fact, numerous people never interact with AWS except through the Console — it's that powerful. This part introduces you to the Console, steps you through setting up your own special AWS account, and even provides your first taste of cloud computing. You get to interact with AWS's S3 storage administration, upload a picture of your decision, and then connect to it over the Internet and show it in your browser. How fun is that?

I provide screen shots of the different screens you see during your introduction to the Console so that you know exactly what you should see and do. By the end of this part, you'll be prepared to associate with AWS and, more importantly, to learn all about AWS's great computing services. Amazon refreshes the Management Console screens fairly fre☐uently, so the screen captures in this book may appear to be unique than what you see displayed on your terminal. Fortunately, it's usually pretty easy to map functionality starting with one screen form then onto the next, however I needed to provide a heads-up before you get worried about seeing a display that looks different from what's in the book. The Management Console display changes are a side impact of the rapid advancement and innovation within AWS.

Setting Up Your Amazon Web Services Account

The first thing to do is to make your very own AWS account. In this multistep process, you sign up for the administration, give your billing information, and then affirm your concurrence with AWS to make your account. Are you game? How about we bounce right in:

1. Point your favorite web program to the fundamental Amazon Web Services

page at http://aws.amazon.com.

You ought to see a screen.

On the next screen, you're given the opportunity to sign in with a existing AWS

99

account or set up a new account. You're setting up another account.

In fact, you can also use your existing Amazon retail account if you have one, despite the fact that I don't prescribe that. Think about it — if you share your AWS account and use a retail identifier for it, down the line someone you're sharing your AWS with may end up purchasing a decent big flatscreen TV on your dime. So my suggestion is that you set up another AWS account.

3. Make sure that the I Am a New User radio button is selected, fill in an appropriate e-mail address in the given field, and then click the Sign In Using Our Secure Server catch.

AWS takes you to a new page, where you're asked to enter your login credentials.

4. Enter a username, your e-mail address (twice, just to be sure), and the password you want to use (again, twice, just to be certain).

5. Snap Continue button.

Doing so brings up the Account Information screen, asking for your address and phone number information. You're asked to select the crate confirming that you agree to the terms of the AWS customer agreement.

6. Enter the required personal data, affirm your acceptance of the customer

understanding, and then click the Create Account and Continue button.

The following page asks you for a credit card number and your charging address data. Amazon has to be sure to get paid, right?

7. Enter the re⬚uired installment data in the suitable fields and then Click Continue.

The following page you see is a bit inquisitive looking. Amazon needs to confirm your personality, so it requests a phone number it can use to call you.

8. Enter your telephone number in the proper field and click the Call Me Now catch. AWS displays a stick code on the

screen and then calls you on the phone number you supplied.

9. Pick up the telephone and enter the displayed PIN code on the telephone keypad.

The AWS screen updates to look like.

10. Click the Continue button.

You're requested to hold up a bit to have your record set up by AWS, be that as it may, in my experience, this is no more than two or three minutes. You'll at that point be sent a e-mail confirming your account setup; you need to click on a connection in that email to finish the account information exchange process.

After setup is complete, you should see a screen that records all the services you're already signed up for automatically, just by creating your account. Very an amazing list, eh?

Here are two important points to take away from this initial account setup:

✓ Your account is now set up as a general AWS account. You can use AWS resources anyplace in the AWS system — the US East or either of the two US West regions, Asia Pacific (Tokyo, Singapore, or Australia), South America (Brazil), and Europe (Ireland). Put another way, your account is scoped over the aggregate of AWS, however resources are situated inside a specific region.

√ You have given AWS a credit card number to pay for the assets you use. As a result, you have an open tab with AWS, so be careful about how much computing resource you consume. For the purposes of this book, you don't have to stress much over expenses — your initial sign-up provides a free level of administration for a year that should be sufficient for you to perform the steps in this book as well as experiment on your own without breaking your piggy bank.

On the off chance that you're worried about overspending on AWS, Amazon's got your back. You can set a charging alert with a specified amount you don't want to go over; if your AWS total use for a month approaches that number, Amazon will send you an alert. You can empower charging alerts by clicking My Account in the Management Console landing page and then clicking on Account Activity on the subse uent page.

That's it. You're all set up in AWS and ready to start cloud computing. In the event that you're anything like me, you're eager to go for somewhat of a spin, just to see how AWS works. So prepare to do one small task with AWS — store and recover a photo from the AWS object storage administration knows as S3.

You start by going to the AWS home page and placing the cursor over the My Account/Console button in the upper-right corner of the screen. You should see a menu displayed underneath the cursor.

Snap the top thing listed: AWS Management Console. You then see a page that provides access to all the services you're marked up for, including S3. (You may have to enter your password again to get to the Management Console from the pull-down menu).

The pull-down menu on the left side of the page allows you to characterize your AWS Management Console start page. (It's right there under the Set Start Page heading.) The default is the general landing page, although you can choose any one of the specific pages associated with a particular AWS administration. For now, leave your start page as is.

Education Foundation on AWS

Do you have to be a huge organization, like Netflix or Amazon, to take advantage of AWS? Not at all. Let me share a case study I was personally included in: the Silicon Valley Education Foundation (SVEF). Not at all like Amazon.com or Netflix, SVEF is a little organization — it has less than 30 employees. Furthermore, unlike Amazon.com or Netflix, SVEF isn't a sophisticated technology user; however its mission focuses on helping students with indispensable science, technology, building, and math (STEM) skills, its staff isn't strong on IT aptitudes.

SVEF engaged the technology consulting firm I ran at the time to evaluate one of its most critical applications, designed to let teachers contribute, share, and improve lesson plans for their classes. SVEF had connected with an outside firm to design and fabricate the application; it evaluated whether the infrastructure on which the application was running was powerful enough to avoid downtime and could support enormous growth in traffic, which SVEF expected as more teachers embraced the application.

Getting to Your First AWS Service

After you're the proud owner of an AWS account, it's time to do something helpful. Start by checking out your S3 assets. To do so, click the S3 interface on your AWS Management Console start page.

You're taken to a page that lets you manage your S3 resources. In the event that you have sharp eyes, you'll ⬚uickly see that there's nothing listed on the page. So the first thing you have to do is create a capacity resource where you can place your first object.

Before I walk you through the step-by-step process of making a storage resource, though, I want to talk a bit about terminology. You'll notice on the left side of the S3 screen is a catch labeled Create Buckets. Now, you may wonder why something that sounds like you'd get it at a hardware store is prominently displayed in AWS. The answer is simple: AWS refers to all top level identifiers within S3 as buckets, signifying, you may presume, a spot to put stuff to store. (The term basin is, perhaps, your first exposure to AWS's curious nomenclature, however I assure you it won't be the last!)

That the entire application was hosted on a solitary server in a colocation office made the appropriate response self-evident: The application wasn't secured against hardware failure, had no redundancy, and would face significant challenges if application use scaled significantly.

We played out a study comparing three choices:

Introduce extra hardware to implement redundancy; implement virtualization to abstract the application from specific hardware and make it simple to migrate to new hardware in instance of failure; and use Amazon Web Services.

Our conclusion, based on both economics and the shortage of IT aptitudes within the SVEF organization, was that SVEF should move its application to AWS. SVEF would save money running on AWS, compared to its ongoing hosting expense.

It would likewise endure no more than ten minutes of downtime if the AWS equipment were to fail. What's more, finally, if the application required more resources as a result of overwhelming use, it would be trivially simple to shut down one application instance and start another, bigger one.

Based on this proposal, SVEF moved its application to AWS, where it has run happily ever since and with little downtime. Inspired by the success of moving this application to AWS, SVEF evaluated all the applications it was running, and inside a half year migrated all of them to cloud situations.

So even if your organization isn't a goliath of technology, you can still use AWS and advantage from it.

The first thing to do, accordingly, is to create a can. Before you run out and do so, however, keep a couple AWS conditions in mind:

✓ Bucket names must be uni◻ue within the entire AWS system. The names must be novel across all client accounts. So if I have a pet named Star and choose to name one of my containers Star in his honor, and somebody else has already named one of her basins Star, well, I'm out of luck. This isn't terribly helpful, yet that is the way it is.

✓ Although bucket names are worldwide (unique across the whole AWS system, in other words), buckets themselves are found in a particular area. Suppose you need a bucket to reflect your organization's name — Corpname, for model. In the event that you use Corpname to create a bucket, you'll isolate that name to a solitary region, even if you want to place objects throughout the world in a bucket associated with your company's name. So, a superior strategy is to use a typical identifier with district explicit information as part of the bucket name; for example, you can use

Corpname-US-East for a bucket in the eastern US area and Corpname-US-West-Oregon for a can in the district associated with Oregon.

✓ Use all lowercase letters in making a bucket. Even though the authority S3 naming principles let you use uppercase letters, the S3 Management Console doesn't allow them for cans created in most AWS regions. On the off chance that you try to include uppercase letters in the bucket name, the Console returns an mistake message. Keep in mind that, although AWS is a wonderful service, it does have its peculiarities. You can always find a way around them, yet don't be amazed when you keep running into things that don't work just the way AWS says they will.

Enough about terminology and naming shows — it's time to make your first basin:

1. On the S3 home page, click the Create Bucket catch.

Doing so brings up a screen similar to the one you see.

2. Enter a name for your bucket in the Bucket Name field.

Since this is only a test, feel free to choose any name you like — and don't stress — if it's a basin name that's already in use, AWS lets you know.

3. Choose an area from the Region pull-down menu.

Choose the "Oregon" thing.

4. Click the Create catch.

AWS makes your new bucket and returns you to the S3 page for managing your assets. There, you see something, which now lists the bucket you just created.

Congrats! You've now done your first bit of cloud registering. Obviously, it's not useful yet — your bucket just sits there, like a empty filing bureau, so put something into it so that you can see how it all hangs together.

Stacking Data into S3 Buckets

I recommend that for your first S3 experiment, you upload a picture that you can then retrieve and see showed in your program. You start out on the S3 page for managing your resources.

Look for the bucket you just made. Found it? Good!

1. Click to select the bucket you made.

Doing so opens the bucket, and the right side of the screen records a number of activities you can take inside the bucket.

2. Snap the Upload button.

The Upload-Select Files discourse box appears.

3. Snap the Add Files catch.

4. Using the file selector gadget that appears, browse your nearby record system, select a file to upload, and then click Open at the bottom of the widget.

You return to the Upload-Select Files dialog box.

5. Snap the Start Upload button in the base right corner of the dialog box.

Following a couple of moments, your bucket lists the file you just uploaded. In the event that you click on the Properties button on the upper right, you'll see data on the file.

Uploading the record is half the fight. Presently all you have to do, via a browser, is access the picture you just uploaded. Before you can do that, however, you need to set consents on the object to make it available over the Internet to someone other than the proprietor (that is you, by the way). To do that, follow these steps:

1. In the listing of transferred records, click to select the file you just uploaded.

2. Click the Properties button in the upper-right corner of the screen.

Doing so brings up a pane loaded up with all kinds of information about the selected object. You can also get to a file's Properties information by right-clicking a selected file and picking Properties from the menu that appears.

3. Click the bolt next to Permissions.

The Permissions section expands to show the Permissions data. You ought to see only yourself listed next to Grantee as somebody capable to get to the document. You need to include a consent so that others can access the document as well.

4. Click the Add More Permissions connect.

An extra drop-down menu (labeled Grantee as well) appears below the first menu.

5. Choose Everyone from this second drop-down menu, select the associated Open/Download check box, and then click Save.

The record is now accessible to everyone. To get to it, you only have to track down the URL you want to use.

6. Go back to the Properties screen.

Here you will see a panel of information on the object, including its URL.

7. Duplicate the URL listed in the Link section, create a new tab in your browser, enter the URL you just copied into the address line, and hit Enter.

S3 URL Naming Conventions

On the off chance that you take a closer look at the URL, you see that it follows an unusual naming convention. The domain is amazonaws.com, however to the left of the domain is s3-us-west-1. You can probably figure out that it represents the region in which you chose to create your bucket. AWS prepends provincial information to its domain in order to direct re?uests to get to the object. DNS can then efficiently and reliably locate the overall resource storing an S3 object.

To one side of the domain is the name of the bucket you created. The bucket name is part of every re?uest to S3 and is included in the URL. Following the bucket name in the URL is the filename of the actual object. For the situation of my model, it's the not-very sharp name Cat Photo. (Note that S3 replaces spaces in a filename with plus signs.)

A container can contain just files. It's conceivable to make folders within a bucket to allow better organization of files. Truth be told, folders can contain organizers themselves, thus allowing S3 to impersonate the shows of computer file systems.

AWS presents the association of S3 as a set of buckets containing objects or folders, which can contain other organizers or objects.

Final Words on the AWS Management Console

You've accomplished a lot in this chapter: You've become familiar with the AWS Management Console, set up your own AWS account, and even chalked up your first AWS experience by experimenting with the S3 storage service.

I trust that this information has helped you understand how simple it is to get started with AWS. In the event that you followed the step-by-step instructions in this chapter, you likely spent no more than 30 minutes on them, from composing aws.amazon.com in a browser address window to getting to your first cloud computing resource. I also trust this first taste of AWS has whetted your hunger to study it, on the grounds that I dive next into the full panoply of AWS administrations.

Things are not what they seem

Keep in mind that although the S3 Management Console presents files in a nice, neat folder structure, there is in fact no progressive organization of questions inside S3 basins. It's just a collection of articles spread throughout S3, with arbitrarily complex asset names that contain shows, as the slash (/), as a component of the resource name. S3 is referred to as a flat storage framework, which means that all objects reside at the top level, with those resource names appearing to reflect hierarchy, however in fact being nothing yet a S3 naming convention.

It's hard to wrap your head around this idea, yet it provides AWS with enormous flexibility and adaptability.

Because no hierarchical association is truly present, AWS can add stockpiling ability to an about unending degree and include it without upsetting what's already in the S3 system. This clever game plan takes some getting used to, given how most people are natural with file systems reflecting progressive organization.

AWS Platform Services

Amazon Web Services (AWS) gives you the center services S3, EC2, and Amazon EBS and then all the additional administrations such as IAM, ELB, and Route 53. The AWS stage administrations, be that as it may, are the focal point of this section — they dial up the level of sophistication, by concentrating on these three territories of functionality:

✓ Services that provide extra application functionality: For model, Amazon's Simple Queue Service (SQS) gives functionality to enable nonconcurrent communication between your application and its users or perhaps another application. I call them extended services.

✓ Additional applications that commoditize traditional software contributions that are important however have typically been expensive and complex: A example is the recently launched Redshift business intelligence application. Numerous established merchants possess this space, and their applications have two characteristics in common: They cost a lot, and they're troublesome to use. Redshift aims to streamline the building and running of a business intelligence application and to make it much less expensive to work.

✓ AWS management tools: The AWS API and Management Console are useful for overseeing specific AWS administrations (individual EC2 instances, for example), however they don't provide much help in managing a aggregation of AWS assets that make up a application. How can you define and manage the collection of assets that comprise your application? Amazon offers three separate tools: Elastic Beanstalk, CloudFormation and OpsWorks. You should comprehend the differences between them so that you can select the right one.

AWS platform administrations offer the same benefits (and generate the same problems) as the center administrations. Though they provide useful, easy-to-use functionality at a sensible price, they present the potential for lock-in — the venture of so numerous assets in a solution that changing course is nearly impossible. Truth be told, the lock-in potential is probably greater for platform services because they're all the more firmly tied to the AWS environment than many of the extra AWS services talked about in Chapter 8. Accordingly, you must cautiously assess whether the benefit you get by grasping these services exceeds any concerns you may have regarding AWS lock-in.

Searching with CloudSearch

Search is one of the most useful capabilities on the web, and tremendous businesses have been built on search. (Ever hear of Google?) However, not all searches need to cover the entire Internet, and a few quests shouldn't be open.

For example, you may want to make content on your company's site searchable — or limit who can see the outcomes of a pursuit. The challenge for many companies that want to enable search on their websites or other content archives is that the ⍰uality of the typical search apparatuses associated with content management frameworks is, to put it bluntly, awful. The circumstance is worse for organizations that want to make a substance archive — a major collection of documents dropped down into a record system, rather than a actual content the executives system — searchable. These conditions have no search component (no matter how flawed) available.

Traditionally, if you wanted to make a complex search capacity available for your content, whether contained in a content management system or plopped down in a disorganized content archive, your options were unappealing:

✓ Buy costly proprietary search software and use it to organize search capabilities for your substance. This option re⊠uires a large financial cost and bodes well only for high-esteem content.

✓ Download and use open source search software, which is both skilled and inexpensive. This alternative makes search financially reasonable for content that isn't necessarily high-esteem however can be made more useful with search capabilities. The downside is that you still have to

✓ Locate equipment on which to install the search programming. You may have to buy hardware to support your search software.

✓ Install and configure the search software on the equipment you obtain. You need to have detailed knowledge of the hunt programming. Most people have little expertise in this arcane area, however it can't be avoided if you want to empower search on your substance.

✓ Manage the hardware and software to guarantee that your search programming remains up and running. On the off chance that your content repository grows to the point that the files related with it outgrow the hardware you obtained initially, you're back to the same (unappetizing!) purchase equipment and-design the-product routine you began with.

Obviously, this situation is unsatisfactory — and ripe for disruption. Amazon, sensing an opportunity, launched CloudSearch early in 2012. CloudSearch is based on technology that Amazon utilizes on its possess site, which should demonstrate its capability as well as its adaptability.

CloudSearch is based on A9, a pursuit company that Amazon brooded a number of years ago, when it realized that the ability to search — and search accurately — would be important to its business. A9 is used for searching on Amazon and its auxiliaries. Though the original A9 focused on text search and significant results, the A9 technology team has branched out to image search and social pursuit, a category that depends on user interaction to add context to customary text search.

CloudSearch is capable of looking through organized content, such as word processing files, and unstructured content — usually referred to as free text, or unstructured collections of content like web pages or gathering posts. Utilizing CloudSearch is relatively clear, however a bit tricky to get it. The content you want to look has to be indexed (the information within the content is evaluated so that individual words can be located) so that indexes about the word (as well as the documents related with the word) can be built. For model, if you need to be able to search a large number of documents about zoos, you have to assemble an index so that in a hunt for the word elephant, the search software can return every document containing the word elephant.

You upload the information you want to search into a CloudSearch domain, where the given domain name is the name of an accessible documents database. For data transfers, CloudSearch utilizes SDF (short for Search Data Format). Despite the fact that CloudSeach can make SDF on the fly for particular kinds of data, such as PDF and Word files, for others you have to make the SDF documents yourself in order to transfer your information. SDF documents can be formatted in either XML or JSON — two common principles for depicting information accumulations. A SDF record is nothing more than an organized set of key-value items portraying the data you need to be able to search on.

After you upload the SDF archives, CloudSearch analyzes them and creates indexes of all the items you've indicated you want to be capable to search on. For example, if you create a set of SDF documents outlining all players in a game for a given year, you may search on the position played or the number of games played in the year. CloudSearch creates lists on all fields you recognize as accessible. Then you can execute searches against your space on the fields you've identified as searchable. You must additionally make access policies, which are similar to to EC2 security groups. You define the IP delivers that you need to allow access to CloudSearch, for both search access and area authoritative access.

(Typically, you'd allow all IP addresses to search through CloudSearch because the most normal use case is allowing visitors to a site to search information on the site, yet you may restrict search access to employees of your company or a modest number of partners.)

Though you can execute searches from the AWS management reassure, the most common search is directed by means of the CloudSearch API or the CloudSearch CLI (command-line interface). In the event that you're adding search capabilities to a website, you use the API strategy to perform look on your CloudSearch area.

CloudSearch assets

CloudSearch keeps up a high performance level by keeping all records you've created inside the memory of EC2 examples. Now, the obvious question is precisely how many EC2 instances will the CloudSearch domain require?

This number, however, isn't one that you control; AWS consequently calculates how many instances your search domain requires and their size. CloudSearch supports three instances sizes: Small, Large, and Extra Large. On the off chance that reСuired, CloudSearch parts your area files across multiple instances in request to retain them in memory and support fast search performance.

CloudSearch scope

CloudSearch is provincially scoped, which affects where you deploy your CloudSearch domain. On the off chance that the site you're empowering with CloudSearch is in a particular district, there's no fee for network traffic if your CloudSearch domain resides in the same area. Of course, given that CloudSearch is accessible via an AWS API, searches can be executed from anywhere on the Internet, as well as within other AWS regions.

CloudSearch cost

Here are the hourly case prices:

✓ Small search: $.10 per hour

✓ Large search: $.39 per hour

✓ Extra Large search: $.55 per hour

Also, here are the data transfer prices per month:

✓ First 10TB: $.12 per gigabyte

✓ Next 40TB: $.09 per gigabyte

✓ Next 100TB: $.07 per gigabyte

The issue of traffic prices may not be noteworthy, because indexed lists return text documents (both XML and JSON are content based), which do not re🯂uire much network traffic to send, so your traffic charges will presumably not be that high.

You face incidental charges for batch uploads and re-indexing, which shouldn't add significantly to your overall CloudSearch bill. Overseeing Video Conversions with Elastic Transcoder Elastic Transcoder, a relatively new service (began in 2013), is conceptually 🯂uite basic: It changes over video documents from one format to another.

PBS runs on AWS (CloudSearch)

On the off chance that you've joined the Downton Abbey craze on open television, you know how well known PBS is. PBS presents ⬚uality programming on public TV stations all through the United States, and it's renowned as the home of numerous highbrow British dramatic series. Part of the PBS methodology is to complement successful series with extra material and video content so that it can build more loyal spectators and increment viewership.

PBS offers gushing video on the web; in addition, over the recent years it has begun to offer streaming video to portable devices like portable phones and tablets. For all the video PBS serves up, it uses AWS. PBS not just uses EC2 and S3 for processing and facilitating videos yet additionally influences

CloudFront to circulate video content — up to a petabyte of content every month.

More recently, as part of an initiative to more profoundly support mobile devices, PBS has placed extra emphasis on creating versatile applications. Part of this mobile activity requires better-quality looking to enable users on constrained structure factors to still be able to find and enjoy targeted video content. As part of this mobile activity, PBS uses ElasticSearch to enable search. ElasticSearch offers more prominent scalability and better performance, and it frees PBS personnel from having to oversee search software and infrastructure.

Video transcoding is a widely applied computing task. You'd have to have been living under a rock not to have observed that video is everywhere. Though people have used devoted video-recording devices for more than 40 years, the ascent of smartphones (initiated by the dispatch of the iPhone in 2007) has supercharged the video pattern. Spurred on by the iPhone and, more recently, the iPad, video-enabled cell phones and tablets have flooded the showcase. Amazon even provides a family of tablets branded Kindle Fire. Every one of them is now a video recording device.

The ease of sharing video via video-facilitating administrations has skyrocketed too; at the time this book was written, 72 hours of video were uploaded to YouTube each minute of the day. Though it may appear to be presently and then that every one of the 72 of those hours highlight cats in interesting or endearing videos, the truth is that video is currently a communication medium utilized by all types of organizations for a wide range of purposes — entertainment, education, documentation, proof, and a thousand others.

For numerous video creators, this blast of video presents a embarrassment of riches — so many yield devices are accessible, each of which has its own preferred format, that making all the reuired versions of video to support customer preferences is testing. Thus, transcoding — the conversion of one video format to another — is now a critical capacity for video-producing entities. Being able to take a source video and prepare all the versions required for widely used show devices is presently critical for organizations that want to influence the power of visual communication. AWS has been part of the transcoding blend for a long time. In fact, when Netflix first began its video-streaming administration, AWS was there as part of its video-transcoding strategy. AWS joined with video transcoding is a natural fit: S3 is a great choice to store the original and transcoded forms of a video, and EC2 can naturally host the compute-intensive transformation process. No measurements are available to indicate what percentage of total AWS outstanding burden is represented by video transcoding, yet it's probably a noteworthy portion.

The remaining burden associated with transcoding can be erratic — in truth, contingent upon the organization and the type of recordings it creates, transcoding workloads may vary by as much as 1,000 percent over a given timeframe. On the off chance that your organization is utilizing AWS for transcoding purposes, the service might be immaculate from an simple entry purpose of view, however such exceptionally variable workloads force significant management challenges. Translation? You'll likely need to grow and shrink your EC2 processing pool ⬚uite a bit to meet transcoding re⬚uirements.

Given these realities, the launch of Elastic Transcoder was a foregone conclusion: It helps organizations perform useful video transcoding in AWS however removes the management overhead. Versatile Transcoder, which is structured to simplify common transcoding tasks, lets you designate videos that need to be transcoded and automatically pulls singular recordings from S3 stockpiling, performs the transcoding operation, and then places the transcoded versions into S3 storage. Utilizing Elastic Transcoder, you specify the characteristics of the yield format you need for your videos, though it additionally gives a number of preconfigured prevalent yield formats for iPhone, iPad, and, of course, Kindle Fire. You can operate Elastic Transcoder from the AWS Management Console, however it also offers a RESTful interface so that applications can call the service on their own. The RESTful interface is likely to represent the majority of the service's use on the grounds that numerous online video applications will transition to Elastic

Transcoder, given its ease of utilization. Amazon gives language SDKs (programming improvement packs) in various languages such as Python and PHP to reduce the burden on developers; instead of having to call the RESTful assistance legitimately.

Each transcoding job submitted to Elastic Transcoder is represented as a JSON object, containing the name of the pail that holds the document to be transcoded, a set of configurations that you want applied to the file (the yield formats you need, for example), and an area in which to place the transcoded video.

Elastic Transcoder operates quite just:

1. Distinguish the video(s) you need to convert.

2. Create an Elastic Transcoder pipeline or use a current pipeline.

A pipeline in this context is just a help endpoint to which employments are submitted. An AWS account can have a few distinctive pipelines, which allows you to separate and prioritize transcoding errands, if you want. You can, be that as it may, have only one pipeline.

3. Use AWS Identity and Access Management (IAM) to create a role for Elastic Transcoder. This step enables Elastic Transcoder to access your resources (say, video files in S3 cans) to perform transcoding administrations. On the off chance that Elastic Transcoder isn't given appropriate access rights, it cannot access your resources and perform transcoding.

4. (Optional) Create a preset containing the settings that you need Elastic Transcoder to apply during the transcoding process. In the

event that you are utilizing a existing pipeline, you can use an existing preset or create a new preset. Amazon provides presets to support prominent transcoding operations, for example, formatting for the iPhone, which can be used rather than creating your own preset.

5. Create a job, which speaks to the transcoding operation for a specific video. The job is submitted in JSON notation. When the service was initially launched, each output format reЯuired an alternate job; today, you can reЯuest multiple yields in a single job, which reduces your system transfer costs a piece.

6. (Discretionary) Configure Elastic Transcoder to utilize AWS's Simple Notification Service (SNS) to provide you with announcements as the job is executed.

7. After the transcoding job is finished, do something with the output videos stored in S3. You can retrieve the video objects from the S3 buckets in which they've been set, or you can allow access to them from the bucket (with appropriate Access Control List [ACL] settings to permit access, obviously). You can even configure the S3 bucket to serve as a CloudFront origin bucket, which then reserves the video at the AWS CloudFront endpoints.

That's all there is to utilizing Elastic Transcoder. Amazon takes care of managing the service, the instances on which the administration runs, and the queues (pipelines) associated with submitting jobs to the administration. You're only in charge of overseeing the original video file, communicating with Elastic

Transcoder, and doing something with the yield video files. At the end of the day, Elastic Transcoder empowers you to advantage from the process of transcoding recordings without suffering the headache of having to oversee its details.

Flexible Transcoder scope

Elastic Transcoder is regionally scoped: A individual pipeline lives in a single region, although the administration, in light of the fact that it has a RESTful interface, can use S3 basins associated with your account in other regions. At the time this book was written, Elastic Transcoder wasn't available in all AWS regions, though you can expect that Amazon will soon make Elastic Transcoder accessible throughout all AWS areas.

Elastic Transcoder cost

Elastic Transcoder offers ⬚uite a simple cost model: AWS charges a fixed price per minute of transcoded video. For standard-definition (SD) video, the cost is around $.015 per minute; for high-definition (HD) video, the cost is around $.030 per minute. The cost is slightly higher in certain regions, butno SD transcoding (as of this writing) costs more than $.018 per minute, nor does HD transcoding cost more than $.036 every moment.

Amazon offers a free level of Elastic Transcoder use. Every month, the first 20 minutes of SD transcoding, or the first 10 minutes of HD transcoding, is provided for free.

Simple Queue Service

It's time now for my favorite AWS service: Simple Queue Service. (It's a geeky decision, I know — yet what would i be able to state?) The ?ueue is an awesome framework capability, immeasurably underused by most application designers — which is deplorable because you end up with complicated, fragile applications that could be improved if they were incorporated with ?ueue administrations.

Presently that you're without a doubt energized about the line, what exactly is it? The ?ueue concept is dead-easy to understand: It's a correspondence system between two preparing resources that allows them to work together on work without requiring to operate in a synchronous manner. This description may appear complicated, however the fact is that you use ⬚ueues in real-life all the time. Say you need your shirts laundered. You can go to the clothing service, hand over your shirts, hold up around for the service to finish washing and squeezing them, and then take them home. That's one way to do it, however I think you'll concur that it wastes a tremendous amount of your time. You can refer to this mode of activity as synchronous: You call on the clothing service and then wait for it to be complete.

A different way to get your shirts washed — and the way this service gets done universally throughout the world — is that you take your shirts to the clothing, drop them off, get a claim ticket along with a estimate of when to return to pick them up, go do other tasks (which may include dropping off your shoes at a shoe repair place to get new heels introduced), and then return on the estimated preparation date to pick up your decent, crisp, clean shirts.

This second mode is asynchronous. You aren't forced to wait for your shirts to be finished — you just put them into the laundry service's work ?ueue and you get a ticket that is then used to follow the job. You return at the given time, having allowed the laundry to do its work while letting you go off and do other (hopefully) beneficial work.

The ?ueue is the ideal tool for a job that is performed by one service and doesn't re?uire the calling service to wait for the results. Elastic Transcoder, the AWS service I talk about in the prior section "Managing Video Conversions with Elastic

Transcoder," is a good example. Numerous applications that can use video transcoding don't wait for the transcoding process to complete.

Imagine a community site that allows you to upload a video and then makes it available to guests in formats that are convenient to them, such as iPhone, iPad, Kindle Fire, or a webpage. In case you're running the website, you don't want to force users to wait around while videos are transcoded, do you? Especially in light of the fact that the videos being submitted for other people to view, there's no point in making people wait for the transcoding procedure to complete. The video can be submitted and set on the line to be transcoded, leaving the submitter free to do something else (such as investigate the rest of your website).

Many, many processing tasks conform to the offbeat use pattern; as I indication in my Queue Love admission, there are undoubtedly more potential line use cases than aren't taken bit of leeway of by application architects, which is too bad.

Simple Queue Service overview

SQS lets you make a line in AWS and then place and retrieve messages from that line. However, you can likewise set permissions on a ?ueue to allow access to it that is broader than your account. Being able to empower a more extensive population to use your line is useful when you want to allow outside entities, whether a restricted group (say, partners of your company) or the general public, to access it — particularly, being able to submit tasks to your application while not requiring the submitter to wait until the job is complete.

Normally enough, Amazon has designed SQS to be incredibly robust with very high uptime, which forces some plan constraints that, in turn, influence the way SQS operates. You ought to comprehend the operation of SQS to ensure that you aren't taken by surprise by the service's conduct.

SQS allows various message submitters and retrievers to share a ueue, which is an extravagant way to say that you can allow your line to have numerous processes setting messages on the line and removing them. You can, for example, operate a number of AWS instances structured to retrieve uploads of videos for Elastic Transcoder, ensuring that no transcoding re𝑞uest is delayed by an enormous job ahead of it in the line.

One way that Amazon makes SQS robust is that it actualizes redundant 𝑞ueues behind the scenes; if one line fails, another, mirror 𝑞ueue can proceed operating until the bombed line is restarted. This strategy ensures that no resource failure can ever make SQS unavailable. However, because messages may be spread over the redundant assets, they may not be conveyed in the order they were placed on the line. Unlike some other 𝑞ueue products, SQS doesn't ensure first-in, first-out (FIFO) conveyance. In the event that a submitter splits a vocation into a few messages, the receiver cannot be sure that they will be retrieved in the proper order.

In spite of the fact that nonguaranteed delivery order isn't a problem for many line based applications, those that require an arranged se?uence of messages need to create a supra-?ueue coordination mechanism; a se?uence order number that's part of the ?ueue message would be appropriate. A message submitter who places multiple messages that are part of a single overall job may submit a succession request number of one in the first message and an absolute message number of three in that message, indicating to the reader that it needs to receive three messages to make up the entire submission. The receiving application would read the total message number in the first message, perceive that it needs three messages to receive the complete submission, and continue reading until it had retrieved messages two and three.

Despite the lack of a FIFO mechanism. Amazon guarantees that each message is conveyed at least once. Until the message is recovered, it's held in the ⍰ueue, standing by to be read. The potential for messages to be held until they're read can cause a problem if no reader ever re⍰uests a message. In the event that this situation happens often enough, the ⍰ueue can become backed up with unread messages — and with enough unread messages, even AWS can get over-burden. Therefore, SQS has a message time-out period that defines how long a message is retained in the line. The default retention period, set at four days, can be adjusted to meet the re⍰uirements of the application. Another SQS trademark to be mindful of is that ⍰ueue messages remain in the line until they're deleted — notwithstanding when they've been read. AWS does this because, even if a message is perused, it might not be completely acted on — the reading application may crash or generally fail to complete the undertaking associated with the message. To avoid situations in which the line message is read however not fully acted upon due to resource failure, AWS implements a perceivability break: While a message is being read, it's locked for a period to ensure that no other reader can access it. However, one key task for a peruser is to delete the message when the task related with the message is complete; if the reader fizzles to erase the message, another process can — when the visibility time-out expires — read the message again and perform the task associated with the message.

Clearly, redundantly performing work isn't a good idea (generally speaking) and, depending on the application, may even cause problems. Hence, your perusing applications must erase SQS messages after they have finished their undertakings. The message size in SQS is restricted to 64KB — for many applications, maybe not a significant restriction; if the complete task is to place somebody's name in a database, 256KB is probably more than adequate.

On the other hand, you can easily imagine queue-based tasks that can be far larger. In the video transcoding model from prior in this chapter, nearly every video submitted would be far bigger than 64KB. The reason for this size restriction is, once more, to avert SQS from being overloaded with re⬚uests — too many overlarge messages can cause SQS to stifle.

So what can you do to overcome this size restriction? It's straightforward: Rather than place the large information payload (in the model, the enormous video file) in the message, you can, for instance, put it in a S3 bucket. You then place the S3 pail name in the message and place the message in the line. The ⬚ueue reader reads the message and recovers the video from the S3 basin based on the information contained in the message. This aberrant pointer system is well-established and commonly used with SQS.

SQS scope

SQS is regionally scoped. Each ⍰ueue is associated with a particular region; when you make an SQS ⍰ueue, you characterize which AWS region will serve as your ⍰ueue's home. However, because SQS is an AWS-gave service, you don't have to place it in a particular availability zone. In fact, Amazon undoubtedly runs each SQS ⍰ueue in various availability zones to ensure robustness and to prevent disappointment in the far-fetched event of a entire availability zone going offline.

The confinement of an SQS line to a particular region shouldn't be viewed as an issue; each ⍰ueue comes with a URL to which clients can submit jobs from anyplace. Given that AWS doesn't charge for inbound traffic — and therefore no traffic charge is associated with submitting jobs to a SQS ueue — the region restriction of SQS has no huge repercussions.

On the other hand, if you're planning to have an EC2 instance inside your own account submit messages to the SQS ueue, you need the occasions and the ueue to reside in the same region. Otherwise, the EC2 instances incur charges for traffic sent interregionally — even if they're at the smaller interregional cost.

SQS cost SQS costs $.50 per million SQS reuests, where a solicitation is any kind of SQS API call. That means both message submission and retrieval, as well as setting a line attribute and the like would bring about a charge. Naturally, message submission and retrieval represent the tremendous dominance of SQS API calls, so those are the sources of most SQS costs. Up to ten messages (if they're less than the 64KB message limit) can be grouped together to check as just one accommodation.

SQS also offers a free-use level; you receive up to 1 million SQS requests per month for nothing.

Don't overlook that you also pay for traffic sent out of AWS, starting at $.12 per gigabyte and descending as more traffic is sent. The first gigabyte of outbound traffic is free each month.

SQS use

I hope that my introduction to SQS and my overview of the administration arouses your interest in using it. Lines are extremely useful, and SQS is valuable, robust, and extremely cost-effective. The most overwhelming challenge for most people in using 🅀ueues is to think about application structure differently. Or maybe than picture a sequential progression of tasks within an application, with each task waiting on a previous task to be completed, you have to think about how to disconnect two tasks, make it possible for them to convey, and inform one another when work is to be done. Using a 🅀ueue allows a application to avoid all this holding up around and offer a superior user experience — which is important. I urge you to experiment with SQS to see how you can segment your applications into independent substances that use lines to submit tasks to, and retrieve tasks from, each other. After you get the hang of using 🅀ueues, you'll start to see lots of opportunities to use them, and you'll likely reexamine a significant number of your application design choices.

Basic Notification Service

As the saying goes, Simple Notification Service (SNS) does what it says on the can: It sends warnings about a event by means of an advantageous mechanism as a way of alerting an individual or a computer program that something intriguing just happened.

The simplicity of this depiction gives a false representation of the control of notices, be that as it may. Consider the case of a framework chairman who's responsible for the legitimate activity of an application inside AWS. Clearly, if something stops working appropriately, she needs to know immediately.

One way to make the administrator aware of application problems is to have her be logged on to AWS at all times, to obsessively check the condition of the application consistently (which is neither efficient nor fun). Another way is to use a notification: After defining at any rate one condition that the administrator needs to think about (and, presumably, respond to), you create a mechanism to respond to the condition(s). At the point when the mechanism identifies one of these conditions — errors show up on database reads, for model — it sends a notification to one or more people to evaluate the issue and choose whether to take action.

Notifications can be sent in an assortment of ways — via e-mail or SMS messages, for instance. Moreover, notifications don't even have to be sent to humans; they can be sent (via e-mail) to a program that takes action whenever it receives a message with a given subject.

The notification is a straightforward idea yet extremely powerful being used. System administrators swear by them (and, once in a while, at them, such as when they get them at 3 in the morning or while on holiday). You may notice a similarity between SNS and SQS — don't both involve an element submitting a message to a service that then delivers it? Truly, however with SQS, the substance receiving the message has to take action in order to receive it; with SNS, the service sends the message to the accepting entity automatically, with no action required on the part of the receiving element. This concept is referred to as pull versus push: With SQS, the receiving entity needs to pull the information; whereas with SNS, the information is pushed to the receiving substance.

The qualification between pull and push is useful in situations where the event that the receiving element is on the post for is infrequent however extremely important. You wouldn't need a receiving entity surveying a message queue every second for an occasion that happens once a month; it would be extremely expensive in terms of processing to pay for constant polling on the off chance that this month's event will happen in the next second. With a notification service, receiving entities (which, again, can be either people or PC programs) can perform their other work, secure in the knowledge that they'll know nearly immediately when the periodic occasion occurs.

SNS review

I trust that the prior clarifies that notices are extremely useful. On the other hand, they're a fair amount of work to set up and, if a huge volume of warnings are being sent, they can be a ton of work to manage. Sounds like a perfect opportunity for AWS, isn't that so? You are correct. SNS works as an AWS administration that you make inside your account. After you make the service, you're prepared to begin conveying notifications.

You can — and probably will — have different notice streams inside your notification administration. You may have one stream for events and messages from your application to system administrators to alarm them to possible problems with your application. You may have another notification stream for your application to send messages to users of your application. You more likely than not wouldn't need to blend messages for those two very different audiences such that one could read notification messages intended for the other.

SNS allows you to send messages to various audiences (or, indeed, to different individuals within the same audience) by setting up separate topics. A topic, in this context, is a predetermined stream of notifications that one or more entities can publish. I use the term elements on the grounds that the topic distributer can be a software component (say, a database that sends notices whenever certain conditions occur) or a person (someone who signs on to the AWS

Management Console and uses it to send a message, for model). Likewise, the notice beneficiary can be either a human or a product component. Line messages — like the messages in Amazon's SQS service — can be recovered by just one entity; by contrast, notices such as the ones sent by SNS are sent to any entity that is joined to receive notifications about a particular theme.

Clearly, one key re□uirement for (successful) notices is the capacity to control who can send or get notifications — and just because someone needs to get notifications doesn't mean he should.

The method that SNS uses to control who (for sure) can send or receive notifications on a given point is the topic policy. As the owner of the topic, you can create policies to control who can join to send or receive a point's Notifications. (The entities that do the sending or getting are known inside SNS as principals.)

This rundown depicts your decisions for who receives topic notifications:

✓ **Individual:** You can identify by policy specific people within your account who are permitted to send or receive notifications.

SNS is coordinated with AWS Identity and Access Management (IAM) to deal with the individual identities that are SNS principals.

✓ **Accounts:** You can identify AWS accounts that can go about as principals with regard to a specific point. The AWS account identifier is used to denote a account that can act as a principal for the SNS theme.

✓ **Public:** You can permit anyone to act as a principal for your SNS theme. It's probably a bad idea for the open to have the option to send notifications, yet it could very well bode well to permit anyone who is interested in a given topic to receive notifications. Though my SNS models along these lines far focus on technical personnel who may need to receive notifications (such as system administrators), you may like a large audience of individuals who aren't part of your account to be notified of an event. A obvious model is to send an email to all endorsers notifying them of a special offer your organization is making accessible — you would simply publish the notification once, and then every person subscribed would receive a notification.

Speaking of everybody getting a notice, you may ask exactly how notifications can be gotten. SNS is rich in notification convention options:

✓ SMS messages sent to a telephone number: The phone number must be enlisted with SNS, naturally enough, yet SNS can send subject notifications through SMS. (Charges for getting the SMS message apply, of course.)

✓ E-mail sent to a e-mail address: This is a common and popular method of sending notifications. The individual who registers to receive the notification gets them via whatever e-mail application she uses.

✓ HTTP/HTTPS: A web application can get notifications over the general open Internet or through secure HTTP. The assumption is that you have a web-based application getting traffic directed to a URL that's listening on the appropriate port; when a notification is received, the web application displays the message on a web page. Of course, the web-based application doesn't have to display it; it can do any number of other things with the notification, including forwarding it via another protocol or storing it in a database. A decent use case for this notification convention is framework chairmen who need a progressing and constantly refreshed presentation of application and system occasions.

✓ Simple Queue Service (SQS): This hero of the previous section can additionally be a notification recipient. You may wonder why you would need to use SQS as an SNS beneficiary. It bodes well if you consider this situation: You need to be sure that you receive and act on significant notifications. On the off chance that you have an application that must be sure that recipients receive notification of events, how can you be sure that the warnings will occur? After all, email may not reach its destination; SMS (at least in my experience) frequently seems flaky, and it's not simple to be sure that a web application is running at the right time to get a notification.

Using SQS ensures that a notification is available and can be acted on regardless; the queue message remains in the queue (up to the message discard time) for as long as it takes for a second entity to recover the message. The use of SQS as the SNS delivery protocol builds SNS heartiness.

One important requirement to keep in mind with regard to SNS is that any underlying recipient recruits have to be confirmed, to prevent vindictive SNS recruits that can flood the recipient with unwanted notifications or, more awful, impose significant costs (such as SMS fees). Every notice convention requires affirmation from the recipient that they (or it) need to get notices on the topic. This technique can be a piece challenging for nonhuman recipients. For example, a web application still gets an underlying affirmation message from SNS and must be able to get, translate, and react to the message before starting to receive notices. The application's code first must be capable to differentiate between the initial invitation and subse uent notifications and then respond accurately to the greeting. Otherwise, SNS decides that the topic membership was a mix-up and refuses to forward notifications to the application.

SNS scope

SNS is a regionally scoped service. However, SNS works as an AWS administration and is accessible from outside the area; therefore, external programs can use SNS. Each topic, upon creation, is doled out an Amazon Resource Name, or ARN. A entity, either human or application, that needs to publish a notice calls the SNS service with the topic's ARN as one of the contentions. Likewise, notifications can be gotten outside of AWS; SNS forwards them via the selected convention to wherever the notification beneficiary is located.

SNS cost

SNS has probably the most unusual valuing of any AWS service in light of the fact that of the various protocols it supports for notice delivery. The essential service is cost-effective: $.50 per million SNS API demands and you don't pay for the initial million SNS API re?uests per month. However, the cost of the notifications themselves shifts, depending on the protocol:

✓ HTTP/HTTPS ($.06 per 100,000 notices): The initial 100,000 notifications per month are free.

Simple E-Mail Service

Let's face it: E-mail is the hardest-working administration on the Internet. In spite of the fact that people gripe endlessly about it and continually talk about the up-and comers that will make e-mail obsolete (Facebook, anyone?), e-mail proceeds to flood the Internet — and it's growing all the time.

E-mail is an incredibly effective way to communicate. It excels at transmitting huge sums of data (enormous as compared to Twitter, for instance), and it has the prudence of giving a long-lasting record of correspondence, making it easy to refer to a communication from the past or to reinitiate an exchange by sending a previous e-mail.

Past its virtues as a personal correspondence tool, e-mail is an incredible vehicle for business correspondence. Numerous businesses use email to send information to their clients for many purposes — to acknowledge an request, track a package, respond to a Ωuestion, and so on.

When tied to recipient socioeconomics, email can be a powerful marketing tool. You can carry out tightly targeted communication at a fraction of the cost of conventional direct marketing instruments, with email delivery almost instantaneous compared to "snail mail" time spans.

One fly remains in the e-mail ointment, however: managing the email server software. It's finicky, it re☐uires constant configuration and tinkering, and it's troublesome to manage when email traffic can fluctuate fiercely. Companies can use e-mail services, thereby avoiding the management cerebral pain, however the high cost of such services can create other headaches.

So there you have it — a core administration, one with high and profoundly variable loads and one that is difficult to oversee and costly to boot. It sounds like a job for AWS. What's more, Amazon has ventured up to tackle the activity, providing an AWS-based service that provides enormous scalability at a reasonable cost:

Simple Email Service (SES).

SES provides an easy-to-use e-mail service
that can bolster a high volume of email. It
probably wouldn't surprise you to learn that
SES is based on Amazon's own internally
created email application, because Amazon
sends out a ton of email every day. Amazon
merely polished up its existing service so
that it could be utilized as part of AWS.

SES outline

SES is direct, thoughtfully. E-mail is an
entrenched set of guidelines and conventions,
so SES actualizes and bolsters established
email rehearses. SES underpins the Simple
Mail Transfer Protocol (SMTP), a venerable
protocol for sending e-mail. You present
your e-mail to SES, using one of the

supported integration components, and it sends the email to the recipient — simple as pie.

Of course, this basic story has a few confusions, all related to the seductive usefulness of e-mail. Just as companies have discovered e-mail to be a incredibly simple way to engage with customers and prospects, so too have malefactors who send endless amounts of spam. The potential for SES to be used to disseminate spam is 𝌆uite high, with these potentially horrible outcomes for Amazon:

✓ SES can be seen as a haven for spam, which can lead to customers not needing to use SES, or perhaps AWS itself.

✓ In an attempt to limit spam, outside gatherings, such as ISPs, may deny to acknowledge email from AWS on sake of their clients.

✓ If an ISP's refusal to acknowledge email makes SES unusable, honest clients of SES would be unfairly punished for using the same AWS administration as spammers.

Obviously, none of these outcomes is acceptable to Amazon, so it has implemented a number of SES re⬚uirements to avoid issues. Because of these re⬚uirements, beginning and then using SES requires you to deal with these imperatives that are important to comprehend as you prepare to use SES:

1. When you sign up to use SES, you must enlist the area from which you will send email (say, example.com). Amazon

approves your domain registration in a day or two, so be prepared to work on something else while you're waiting. Amazon refers to this process as verifying your domain.

2. After your domain is verified, the individual e-mail addresses from which you'll send email must be verified as well. SES sets a cutoff of 1,000 verified addresses, so the administration is more appropriate for showcasing efforts and application output than for general corporate e-mail support.

3. When you get began, Amazon places you in a SES sandbox, in which you're limited in what addresses you can send e-mail to — these addresses need to be from within your own domain, which prevents you from immediately spamming someone. During

the sandbox period, you're limited to 200 e-mails per day, all of which have to be sent to e-mail addresses that are confirmed by Amazon.

4. At the point when you have established your trustworthiness, Amazon will move you to the Big Leagues: production SES. Even though you're no longer rationed to the sandbox limits, you're not allowed full, free SES use. As you begin, you're limited in the number of e-mails you can send in any single day, and you're limited in how many you can send in any single second. As Amazon gains more confidence in your use of SES, it raises these limits.

AWS offers four different ways to interact with SES and send e-mails:

✓ The AWS Management Console: The reassure allows you to create and send messages. This method, which isn't very efficient, is offered primarily to let you test your SES setup and service.

✓ The SES API: You can write legitimately to the SES API in request to make web administration calls and interact with the SES API interface.

✓ Programming language SMTP modules: SMTP is an admired protocol — most programming languages have modules or libraries that empower the sending of e-mail via SMTP. Note that the utilization of a programming language SMTP module re🔲uires a unique SES username and secret phrase (different from the account username and password), which must be

mentioned by means of the AWS
Management Console.

✓ AWS programming language SDKs:
Amazon itself offers SDK libraries
encapsulating the SES API, which can be
used in writing programs to interface with
SES.

No matter which association method you
use, SES obediently sends off anyway many
messages you tell it to. In addition to
faithfully sending e-mail, SES collects a
number of statistics for you — the number
of messages that were delivered, bounced
(both temporarily and forever), or rejected
and the number of grievances (e-mail
declined by a receiving ISP based on its view
of your e-mail as spam). As for rejected e-
mails, before sending your e-mail, SES
passes it through content channels designed

to weed out spam and content that may be perceived as spam; SES lets you know if any sent message is rejected.

Sending e-mails through a programming module or an AWS SDK is relatively easy. It more often than not calls for setting some variables (the send-to email address, sent from e-mail address, e-mail body content, and the like), and a call to "send" the email to the SMTP service.

Usually, the most difficult part of sending an e-mail is composing the message body — choosing whether it ought to be plain content or HTML, or both, and how to format the body so that the recipient finds it interesting enough to open. SES doesn't help you with that decision, despite the fact that it supports both HTML and plain content e-mail. On the other hand, people tend to futz around with e-mail a great deal, to get the organizing correct, and then don't touch the formatting settings for months (or years). This errand is the place the sandbox comes in handy — it's a place to explore, to be sure that you nail the suitable e-mail plan.

SES scope

SES is regionally scoped and, like all platform services, is open from anywhere on the Internet, so it's 🮲uite conceivable to use SES as a standalone administration, with messages sent from an application residing in your own information center.

SES cost

SES costs $.10 per 1,000 e-mails. In the event that you use EC2 or Elastic Beanstalk, you can send 2,000 messages free per day.

Standard outbound network traffic charges apply to SES messages, which are based on total traffic size. In the event that you send humongous e-mails, you'll rack up more of a charge than if you send small, one-line messages. You're also charged for sending e-mail connections, at the pace of $.12 per gigabyte.

SES considers a e-mail message to be one message sent to one email address. So if you send one e-mail to 100 different recipients, it counts as 100 email messages.

Simple Workflow Service

Simple Workflow Service (SWF) addresses a typical challenge in huge, distributed applications: how to organize all the work between the segments of the application, especially when some of the work carried out by a component may rely upon the successful completion of work by another component. SWF is the commercial offering of a help that Amazon implemented for its possess, internal operations. SWF is a powerful service, yet I would say that the initial letter in the acronym (S for Simple) isn't accurate.

Not at all like most AWS services, SWF isn't straightforward to understand or use. On the other hand, the problems that SWF was designed to address are monstrously complex and without a doubt re☐uire a complex tool to master them. One traditional approach to manage complex workflows is to have a human do it. A person kicks off one task, holds up for it to complete, starts a second task, holds up for it to be done, thus on. This process has a couple very basic problems:

It's slow, and it's boring. It also doesn't scale well. Another technique, used in the past, is to write a custom workflow via scripting or code. That approach definitely addresses the challenges of the past method, yet has its own set of challenges. It underpins the work process it's designed for, however as soon as you want another kind of workflow, well, you're out of luck. Or then again you end up trying to sum up your custom workflow and pretty soon you're working full-time on attempting to keep up your simple workflow product rather than on doing any . . . you know, work.

Obviously, many commercial work process engines are available to solve these two issues. In spite of the fact that these engines are ⬚uite capable, they commonly carry hefty price tags and, given their esoteric nature, aren't simple to get subsidized.

SWF addresses this problem with a general workflow usefulness that's offered and priced like all other AWS services: Use it when you want, and pay for only what you use. On the off chance that you have a complex work process that you need to execute, SWF can be a big help.

SWF diagram

SWF is a generalizable workflow coordinator, commonly called a workflow engine. To use it, you create these two elements:

✓ Decider: Defines the tasks that your work process needs to coordinate

✓ Tasks: Do the work that the decider coordinatesDespite the fact that SWF needs to run in AWS (after all, it's an AWS administration, right?), the tasks aren't limited to running inside EC2. They can run anyplace. In fact, they don't even have to run — a task can be a human-powered thing. For model, if you implement a printing work process, one task can be Review Proof with Client, which is an up close and personal errand. In the wake of accepting positive feedback from the client, the printer's employee can open a web page and click the Approved button for the Review Proof task, and the leftover portion of the work process can proceed in a automated fashion. The workflow need not be a consecutive series of tasks, either; it can handle concurrent tasks that are run in parallel. A workflow can also include task dependencies, in which a given task cannot start until one or progressively past assignments effectively complete.

A SWF decider can incorporate logic to handle task errors and breaks, for example, empowering it to handle problems that occur inside individual tasks. Naturally, you can compose workflows to acknowledge input parameters that control how the work process executes. You can likewise incorporate clocks, signals, and markers in your work process to help coordinate tasks.

Despite the fact that SWF provides an API to collaborate with the service, Amazon has built a fairly full-featured the executives capability into the AWS Management Console. I think it's fair to say that it expects most SWF users to deal with their workflows through the Management Console. SWF can manage workflows that are arbitrarily complex and that might be ⬚uite long-running; therefore, it stores the state of the workflow, which can be gotten to from the AWS Management Console or through the API so that you can decide where things stand with a given workflow execution. Finished work process information is also retained and is available for inspection, in spite of the fact that you may like to erase held information in light of the fact that AWS forces a little charge for retaining completed work process information.

I should caution you: SWF isn't for the faint of heart. In any case, the SWF segment of the AWS Management Console does have a simple application model that shows the power of SWF. This picture preparing application accepts an input image and converts it to sepia or gray-tone, depending on input it gets via a dialog box. To see SWF in action, check out the example.

SWF scope

SWF is provincially checked, despite the fact that it can access AWS assets in other districts also as non-AWS assets.

SWF cost

AWS forces several types of charges for SWF, in spite of the fact that the aggregate cost is extremely low, except if you execute vast numbers of work processes. For every executed workflow, AWS charges $0.0001. However, you receive 1,000 free workflows per month. On the off chance that a work process remains open past 24 hours,

AWS imposes a $0.000005 expense per day. On the off chance that a workflow is retained past fruition, AWS charges the same $0.000005 per day. AWS gives 30,000 open or held workdays for free.

AWS also imposes a fee for individual errands, markers, timers, and signals — $0.000025 per task, signal, timer, or marker. AWS gives 10,000 of these items for free per month. These expenses shift slightly by area, however not significantly.

Dealing with Big Data with the Help of Elastic MapReduce

You have to have been living under a rock not to have heard of the term big information. It's a deceptively straightforward term for an unnervingly difficult problem: how to make sense of the deluges of information flooding into today's applications.

Let me quote a couple factoids to layout the dimension of the big-data challenge. In 2010, Google's administrator, Eric Schmidt, noted that humans now make as much information in two days as all of humanity had made up to the year 2003. Moreover, the research firm IDC projects that the digital universe will arrive at 40 zettabytes (ZB) by 2020, resulting in a 50-overlap development from the beginning of 2010. In other words, there's lots and heaps of information, and its growth is accelerating.

The test that enormous information presents is that most of the established information examination devices can't scale to manage datasets of the size that many organizations want to analyze. For one, traditional business intelligence or data warehousing tools (the terms are used so interchangeably that they're frequently referred to as BI/DW) are extremely expensive; when applied to very large datasets, you soon face national-obligation type numbers.

Amusingness aside, the established BI/DW apparatuses have a more serious scalability shortcoming: They're architected with a central analytics engine that reads data from disks, performs investigation, and spits out results. Today, information sizes are so immense that simply sending the information to be analyzed crosswise over the arrange takes excessively long to perform any useful work. By the time the data is transferred, the bits of knowledge that can be gleaned from it are old.

Clearly, a new BI/DW analytics architecture and issue approach was called for, and for inspiration the industry reached out to Google. Google has actualized a different approach to gathering data. Its architecture, MapReduce, is based on this simple insight: With so much data, it makes sense to move the processing to the information rather than attempt to move the data to the processing. MapReduce takes a very huge datastore that may be spread across hundreds or thousands of machines and formats the information to structure it for the type of analysis you need to perform (that is, it maps the data into an analyzable format), and then you filter the data (reduce the mapped information, in other words) to detach the information you want to examine.

Google treats its MapReduce implementation as exclusive, at the same time, based on a paper it distributed, one person executed a open source version of MapReduce called Hadoop. It's no distortion to state that Hadoop has revolutionized the BI/DW industry. In fact, a entire ecosystem of corresponding items exists to make Hadoop even more helpful.

You've probably already cut to the pursue and recognized a familiar abstain:

Hadoop is valuable, yet complex to install, configure, and manage. Gee, wouldn't it be useful if someone made an simple to-utilize, cost-effective Hadoop solution that integrates with the existing ecosystem, allowing established tools that supplement Hadoop to be used with this administration?

Yes, it would, and Amazon calls its Hadoop solution Elastic MapReduce (EMR). The idea is straightforward:

1. Recognize the data source you want to analyze.

This is data found in S3. EMR can handle petabytes (a petabyte is 1,000 terabytes) of information with no issue.

2. Disclose to EMR how many occasions (and of what type) you want the EMR pool to contain.

EMR can use EC2 standard instances or one of the more exotic types, such as High-IO or High-CPU. Each occasion offers a certain amount of disk storage for running the Hadoop Distributed File System (HDFS).

The total sum of information you need to analyze dictates the number of instances you re?uire.

3. Set up an EMR job flow.

A vocation flow can be either of two types:

• Streaming: Programming language mappers and reducers are presented into

EMR and processed crosswise over EC2 instances and the data they include.

• Query-oriented: A higher-level data warehouse tool, such as Hive (which provides a Structured Query Language-like interface) can be used to run intuitive queries against the information. The output of either type can be stored in S3 and then used for further analysis without requiring an dynamic occupation stream.

4. Continue running the job flow, running MapReduce programs or higherlevel question languages against the data, until you're finished utilizing the job flow. A job flow can be terminated, which terminates all occurrences that make up the EMR pool.

Amazon manages the examples within the EMR pool. In the event that a instance ends out of the blue, Amazon starts a new instance and ensures that it has the right data on it to replace the terminated instance. Furthermore, of course, Amazon takes care of starting the EMR pool, connecting the instances to one another, and running MapReduce programs or providing higher-level tools for you to use for analysis.

EMR bolsters these programming dialects: Java, Ruby, Perl, Python, PHP, R, Bash, and C++. With respect to these higher-level apparatuses, Amazon provides a wide variety. Likewise to Hive (as just mentioned), Amazon also offers Pig (a particular Hadoop language). Finally, on the off chance that you need, you can use EMR to output data that can then be brought into a specific analytics tool like (the curiously named) R.

EMR is one service in which Amazon's pay-only-for-what-you-use philosophy may not be ideal, because transferring and organizing very large datasets to the EMR EC2 instances may take a long time. When you end a job flow, the occurrences on which the EMR pool is running are terminated and the data discarded. The next time you need to run an analysis, you have to rebuild the EMR pool. So you need to establish a trade-off, to balance the cost of keeping your EMR pool up and running versus the cost of modifying it. Clearly, if you plan to run multiple analyses after some time against a data pool, it most likely makes sense to keep your job flow dynamic.

One interesting characteristic of EMR is that it varies from the other platform services I've already described. The others are "helper" services — useful administrations that help you assemble better applications more Ꝗuickly. By differentiate, EMR represents a stand-alone application that's not expected to support an application that the user is writing. Another example of this type of "nonhelper" independent application is Redshift, covered next. I expect that you'll see more of these stand-alone applications, for these reasons:

✓ Its genuine notoriety: Amazon feels that AWS is now accepted as a serious IT player, and IT is willing to trust it with significant use cases. The company is now ready to branch out into regions that provide more direct user benefit in expansion to its built up infrastructure parts that empower users to build their claim applications.

✓ The opportunity to expand: Amazon perceives many application domains as ready for computerization and commoditization. As it gives offerings in these spaces, its clients increasingly benefit, and AWS can become more valuable to them, accordingly cementing its place as a critical part of their IT conditions.

✓ Strategic estimating strategies: AWS recognizes that the high price of current contributions in these application domains counteracts many potential users from taking preferred position of them; its contributions democratize access to these domains. I'll give you a chance to choose whether Amazon is acting simply unselfishly in this regard, or perhaps with an element of self-interest.

EMR scoping

EMR is provincially scoped. You should locate your EMR use in the same area where your information lives, if you want to avoid data transfer fees. (Given the kind of information volumes that EMR supports, avoiding these expenses can be a big deal.)

EMR cost

The primary cost of EMR is the cost of the EC2 instances on which your EMR pool runs, as well as the S3 stockpiling for your input information and results (assuming, reasonably, that you output results to S3).

In addition, you pay an additional EMR fee per instance. Think of it as an instance extra charge that Amazon imposes to manage the EMR service, introduce and configure the EMR programming on the instances inside your EMR pool, and transfer data between all the occurrences and S3. The EMR surcharge is roughly 25 percent of the instance cost, making it (in my opinion, at least) a modest cost for such an amazing application, compared to the cost of managing Hadoop on your own.

Distributed
computing

What is Cloud Computing?

Distributed computing is the on-demand conveyance of figure power, database storage, applications, and other IT resources through a cloud services platform via the Internet with pay-as-you-go pricing. Whether you are running applications that share photos to millions of mobile clients or you're supporting the critical tasks of your business, a cloud services platform gives rapid access to flexible and low-cost IT resources. With cloud computing, you don't need to make large forthright investments in equipment and spend a lot of time on the heavy lifting of overseeing that equipment. Instead, you can provision exactly the right type and size of computing resources you need to power your freshest bright idea or work your IT office. You can get to as numerous assets as you need, in a split second, and pay for what you use.

Cloud computing gives a simple approach to access servers, stockpiling, databases and a broad set of application administrations over the Internet. A cloud services platform, such as Amazon Web Services, claims and maintains the network-connected hardware re?uired for these application services, while you provision and use what you need by means of a web application.

Six Advantages of Cloud Computing

• Trade capital expense for variable expense – Instead of having to put heavily in information centers and servers before you know how you're going to use them, you can pay only when you devour computing resources, and pay only for how much you consume.

• Benefit from enormous economies of scale – By using cloud processing, you can achieve a lower variable cost than you can get on your claim. Since use from many thousands of customers is aggregated in the cloud, providers, for example, AWS can achieve higher economies of scale, which translates into lower pay as-you-go costs.

• Stop guessing limit – Eliminate guessing on your foundation limit needs. When you make a capacity decision prior to conveying an application, you often end up either sitting on expensive inert assets or managing limited limit. With cloud computing, these problems go away. You can access as much or as little limit as you need, and scale here and there as re🔲uired with only a couple minutes' take note.

• Increase speed and agility – In a distributed computing environment, new IT assets are only a click away, which means that you reduce the time to make those assets available to your engineers from weeks to only minutes. This results in a dramatic increment in dexterity for the association, since the cost and time it takes to experiment and develop is significantly lower.

• Stop spending money running and maintaining information centers – Focus on ventures that differentiate your business, not the infrastructure. Distributed computing lets you focus on your claim customers, rather than on the heavy lifting of racking, stacking, and powering servers.

• Go global in minutes – Easily deploy your application in multiple regions around the world with only a couple clicks. This means you can give lower latency and a better experience for your clients at minimal cost.

Types of Cloud Computing

Cloud processing provides designers and IT offices with the capacity to center around what matters most and avoid undifferentiated work such as procurement, maintenance, and capacity planning. As cloud computing has grown in popularity, a few different models and deployment procedures have developed to help meet specific needs of different clients. Each type of cloud service and deployment method gives you with different levels of control, flexibility, and management. Understanding the contrasts between Infrastructure as a Service, Platform as a Service, and Software as a Service, as well as what deployment techniques you can use, can help you choose what set of services is right for your needs.

Cloud Computing Models

Foundation as a Service

Infrastructure as a Service (IaaS) contains the fundamental building blocks for cloud IT and typically provide get to to networking features, computers (virtual or on committed hardware), and data storage space. IaaS provides you with the highest level of adaptability and management control over your IT assets and is most comparative to existing IT resources that numerous IT divisions and developers are familiar with today.

Platform as a Service (PaaS)

Stage as a Service (PaaS) expels the need for your association to manage the basic infrastructure (usually hardware and operating systems) and allows you to focus on the deployment and the board of your applications. This helps you be more efficient as you don't need to worry about resource procurement, capacity planning, software upkeep, patching, or any of the other undifferentiated heavy lifting involved in running your application.

Software as a Service (SaaS)

Software as a Service (SaaS) gives you a completed product that is run and managed by the service provider. In most cases, individuals referring to Software as a Service are alluding to end-user applications. With a SaaS offering you do not have to think about how the service is maintained or how the hidden framework is managed; you only need to consider how you will use that specific piece of software. A typical example of a SaaS application is web-based email which you can use to send and receive email without having to oversee include increments to the email item or keep up the servers and working systems that the email program is running on.

Cloud Computing Deployment Models

Cloud

A cloud-based application is completely deployed in the cloud and all parts of the application keep running in the cloud. Applications in the cloud have either been created in the cloud or have been migrated from an existing foundation to take advantage of the benefits of distributed computing. Cloud-based applications can be built on low-level infrastructure pieces or can use higher level administrations that provide abstraction from the management, architecting, and scaling necessities of core infrastructure.

Cross breed

A hybrid deployment is a way to connect infrastructure and applications between cloud-based resources and existing resources that are not located in the cloud. The most basic method of hybrid sending is between the cloud and existing on-premises infrastructure to broaden, and develop, an association's infrastructure into the cloud while connecting cloud resources to the internal framework. For more data on how AWS can help you with your hybrid deployment, please visit our hybrid page.

On-premises

The deployment of assets on-premises, utilizing virtualization and resource the executives apparatuses, is now and again called the "private cloud." On-premises deployment doesn't provide many of the benefits of cloud computing however is sometimes looked for for its capacity to provide dedicated resources. As a rule this deployment model is the same as inheritance IT framework while utilizing application management and virtualization technologies to attempt and increase asset utilization.

Security and Compliance

Security

Cloud security at AWS is the most elevated priority. As an AWS client, you will benefit from a data center and arrange architecture worked to meet the re uirements of the most security-sensitive associations. Security in the cloud is much like security in your on-premises data centers—only without the costs of maintaining facilities and equipment. In the cloud, you don't have to manage physical servers or storage devices. Rather, you use software-based security tools to monitor and secure the flow of information into and of out of your cloud resources.

A preferred position of the AWS Cloud is that it allows you to scale and innovate, while maintaining a secure situation and paying just for the services you use. This means that you can have the security you need at a lower cost than in a on-premises environment.

As an AWS customer you inherit all the best practices of AWS approaches, architecture, and operational processes built to fulfill the re◻uirements of our most security-sensitive customers. Get the flexibility and agility you need in security controls.

The AWS Cloud enables a shared responsibility model. While AWS manages security of the cloud, you are responsible for security in the cloud. This means that you retain control of the security you choose to execute to protect your own content, platform, applications, systems, and networks no uniquely in contrast to you would in an on-site information center.

AWS furnishes you with direction and expertise through online resources, faculty, and partners. AWS provides you with warnings for current issues, in addition to you have the opportunity to work with AWS when you encounter security issues.

You get access to hundreds of tools and features to help you to meet your security objectives. AWS provides security-specific devices and features crosswise over network security, configuration management, get to control, and data encryption.

Finally, AWS situations are continuously audited, with confirmations from accreditation bodies crosswise over topographies and verticals. In the AWS environment, you can take advantage of automated apparatuses for asset inventory and privileged access reporting.

Benefits of AWS Security

- **Keep Your Data Safe:** The AWS framework puts strong shields in place to help protect your protection. All data is put away in profoundly secure AWS data centers.

- **Meet Compliance Requirements:** AWS oversees dozens of compliance programs in its infrastructure. This means that fragments of your consistence have already been completed.

- **Save Money:** Cut costs by using AWS data centers. Maintain the highest standard of security without having to oversee your own facility

- **Scale Quickly:** Security scales with your AWS Cloud usage. No matter the size of your business, the AWS foundation is planned to keep your information safe.

Consistence

AWS Cloud Compliance empowers you to understand the robust controls in place at AWS to maintain security and data assurance in the cloud. As frameworks are built on top of AWS Cloud infrastructure, compliance responsibilities will be shared. By tying together governance-focused, review inviting service features with applicable compliance or review principles, AWS Compliance enablers manufacture on conventional projects. This causes customers to set up and operate in an AWS security control environment.

The IT framework that AWS gives to its customers is designed and managed in alignment with best security rehearses and a variety of IT security gauges. The following is a partial list of affirmation programs with which AWS goes along:

- SOC 1/ISAE 3402, SOC 2, SOC 3

- FISMA, DIACAP, and FedRAMP

- PCI DSS Level 1

- ISO 9001, ISO 27001, ISO 27017, ISO 27018

AWS provides clients a wide range of data on its IT control environment in whitepapers, reports, confirmations, accreditations, and other outsider attestations. More information is accessible in the Risk and Compliance whitepaper and the AWS Security Center.

Amazon Web Services Cloud Platform

AWS comprises of many cloud administrations that you can use in combinations tailored to your business or organizational needs. This area introduces the major AWS services by class. To access the services, you can use the AWS Management Console, the Command Line Interface, or Software Development Kits (SDKs).

AWS Management Console

Access and manage Amazon Web Services through the AWS Management Console, a simple and intuitive user interface. You can additionally use the AWS Console Mobile Application to quickly see resources in a hurry.

AWS Command Line Interface

The AWS Command Line Interface (CLI) is a brought together tool to manage your AWS administrations. With just one instrument to download and configure, you can control numerous AWS administrations from the command line and automate them through scripts.

Software Development Kits

Our Software Development Kits (SDKs) streamline using AWS services in your applications with an Application Program Interface (API) tailored to your programming language or platform.

Analytics

Amazon Athena

Amazon Athena is an interactive question administration that makes it simple to analyze data in Amazon S3 using standard SQL. Athena is serverless, so there is no framework to oversee, and you pay just for the queries that you run.

Athena is simple to use. Simply point to your information in Amazon S3, define the pattern, and start querying utilizing standard SQL. Most results are delivered inside seconds. With Athena, there's no requirement for complex remove, transform, and load (ETL) occupations to get ready your information for analysis. This makes it easy for anybody with SQL aptitudes to quickly examine large-scale datasets.

Athena is out-of-the-crate integrated with AWS Glue Data Catalog, allowing you to make a bound together metadata archive crosswise over various services, crawl information sources to find outlines and populate your Catalog with new and modified table and partition definitions, and maintain composition forming. You can also utilize Glue's fully-managed ETL abilities to change data or convert it into columnar formats to upgrade cost and improve performance.

AWS Lake Formation

AWS Lake Formation is an assistance that makes it simple to set up a secure data lake in days. A data lake is a centralized, curated, and secured storehouse that stores all your data, both in its original form and prepared for investigation. An information lake enables you to break down information silos and combine distinctive types of investigation to pick up insights and guide better business decisions.

In any case, setting up and managing information lakes today involves a lot of manual, convoluted, and time-consuming tasks. This work incorporates loading data from differing sources, monitoring those data flows, setting up partitions, turning on encryption and overseeing keys, characterizing transformation jobs and monitoring their operation, re-organizing data into a columnar format, configuring access control settings, deduplicating excess information, matching connected records, granting access to data sets, and auditing access over time.

Making a data lake with Lake Formation is as basic as defining where your information resides and what information get to and security policies you want to apply. Lake Formation then gathers and catalogs information from databases and object capacity, moves the data into your new Amazon S3 data lake, cleans and groups information using machine learning algorithms, and secures access to your sensitive data. Your users can then access a unified catalog of information which describes accessible information sets and their proper use. Your users then influence these data sets with their choice of analytics and machine learning services, similar to Amazon EMR for Apache Spark, Amazon Redshift, Amazon Athena, Amazon SageMaker, and Amazon QuickSight.

Amazon Managed Streaming for Kafka (MSK)

Amazon Managed Streaming for Kafka (Amazon MSK) is a fully managed administration that makes it easy for you to build and run applications that use Apache Kafka to process streaming information. Apache Kafka is an open-source stage for building ongoing streaming data pipelines and applications. With Amazon MSK, you can use Apache Kafka APIs to populate data lakes, stream changes to and from databases, and power machine learning and analytics applications.

Apache Kafka clusters are testing to setup, scale, and manage in production. When you run Apache Kafka on your own, you need to provision servers, configure Apache Kafka manually, replace servers when they fail, orchestrate server patches and upgrades, modeler the cluster for high availability, ensure data is durably stored and secured, arrangement monitoring and alarms, and carefully plan scaling events to support load changes. Amazon Managed Streaming for Kafka makes it simple for you to build and run generation applications on Apache Kafka without needing Apache Kafka framework management expertise. That implies you spend less time overseeing framework and more time building applications.

With a couple of snaps in the Amazon MSK console you can create profoundly available Apache Kafka clusters with settings and configuration based on Apache Kafka's deployment best rehearses. Amazon MSK automatically provisions and runs your Apache Kafka clusters. Amazon MSK continuously monitors cluster health and automatically replaces unhealthy hubs with no downtime to your application. In addition, Amazon MSK secures your Apache Kafka cluster by encrypting data at rest.

Application
Integration

AWS Step Functions

AWS Step Functions lets you coordinate various AWS services into serverless workflows so you can fabricate and update applications ?uickly. Using Step Functions, you can design and run workflows that stitch together administrations such as AWS Lambda and Amazon ECS into feature-rich applications. Workflows are made up of a series of steps, with the output of one step acting as input into the next. Application development is less difficult and more intuitive utilizing Step Functions, since it translates your workflow into a state machine diagram that is easy to understand, simple to clarify to others, and easy to change. You can monitor each step of execution as it happens, which means you can identify and fix issues ⬜uickly. Step Functions consequently triggers and tracks each step, and retries when there are errors, so your application executes in request and as expected.

Amazon MQ

Amazon MQ is a managed message broker service for Apache ActiveMQ that makes it simple to set up and operate message brokers in the cloud. Message brokers permit different programming frameworks frequently using distinctive programming dialects, and on various stages to communicate and trade data. Amazon MQ decreases your operational load by overseeing the provisioning, arrangement, and maintenance of ActiveMQ, a well known open-source message dealer. Connecting your current applications to Amazon MQ is simple because it utilizes industry-standard APIs and protocols for messaging, including JMS, NMS, AMQP, STOMP, MQTT, and WebSocket. Using standards implies that in most cases, there's no need to rewrite any messaging code when you migrate to AWS.

Amazon SQS

Amazon Simple Queue Service (Amazon SQS) is a completely managed message queuing service that enables you to decouple and scale microservices, disseminated systems, and serverless applications. SQS eliminates the complexity and overhead related with overseeing and working message oriented middleware, and empowers designers to center around differentiating work. Using SQS, you can send, store, and get messages between software components at any volume, without losing messages or re✷uiring other services to be available. Get started with SQS in minutes using the AWS console, Command Line Interface or SDK of your decision, and three simple commands.

SQS offers two types of message ✷ueues. Standard lines offer maximum throughput, best-effort requesting, and in any event once delivery. SQS FIFO ✷ueues are designed to ensure that messages are processed precisely once, in the exact request that they are sent.

Amazon SNS

Amazon Simple Notification Service (Amazon SNS) is a highly accessible, durable, secure, fully managed pub/sub messaging service that enables you to decouple microservices, distributed systems, and serverless applications. Amazon SNS gives topics for high-throughput, push-based, many-to-many informing. Using Amazon SNS topics, your publisher systems can fan out messages to an enormous number of subscriber endpoints for parallel handling, including Amazon SQS ⊠ueues, AWS Lambda functions, and HTTP/S webhooks. Additionally, SNS can be used to fan out notifications to end users using mobile push, SMS, and email.

Amazon SWF

Amazon Simple Workflow (Amazon SWF) helps developers build, run, and scale background jobs that have parallel or successive advances. You can think of Amazon SWF as a fully-managed state tracker and task coordinator in the cloud. On the off chance that your application's means take more than 500 milliseconds to complete, you need to track the state of processing. On the off chance that you need to recover or retry if an errand fails, Amazon SWF can help you.

AR and VR

Amazon Sumerian

Amazon Sumerian lets you create and run virtual reality (VR), augmented reality (AR), and 3D applications 🗆uickly and easily without requiring any particular programming or 3D designs expertise. With Sumerian, you can build highly immersive and interactive scenes that run on popular hardware such as Oculus Go, Oculus Rift, HTC Vive, HTC Vive Pro, Google Daydream, and Lenovo Mirage as well as Android and iOS mobile devices. For model, you can build a virtual classroom that lets you train new workers around the world, or you can build a virtual environment that enables people to visit a building remotely. Sumerian makes it simple to make all the structure blocks needed to fabricate highly vivid and intuitive

3D experiences including adding objects
(e.g. characters, furniture, and landscape),
and structuring, animating, and scripting
environments. Sumerian does not require
specialized expertise and you can plan
scenes directly from your program.

AWS Cost Management

AWS Cost Explorer

AWS Cost Explorer has an easy-to-use
interface that lets you visualize, comprehend,
and oversee your AWS costs and usage over
time. Get began ⬜uickly by creating custom
reports (counting charts and tabular data)
that break down expense and usage
information, both at a high level (e.g., total
costs and usage across all accounts) and for

profoundly explicit solicitations (e.g., m2.2xlarge costs inside account Y that are tagged "venture: secretProject").

AWS Budgets

AWS Budgets gives you the ability to set custom budgets that alert you when your expenses or usage exceed (or are anticipated to exceed) your planned sum. You can additionally use AWS Budgets to set RI utilization or coverage targets and get cautions when your usage dips under the threshold you define. RI alerts support Amazon EC2, Amazon RDS, Amazon Redshift, and Amazon ElastiCache reservations.

Spending plans can be tracked at the monthly, quarterly, or yearly level, and you can tweak the start and end dates. You can further refine your budget to track costs associated with different measurements, such as AWS service, linked account, tag, and others. Spending alarms can be sent via email and/or Amazon Simple Notification Service (SNS) topic.

Budgets can be created and followed from the AWS Budgets dashboard or via the Budgets API.

AWS Cost and Usage Report

The AWS Cost and Usage Report is a solitary location for accessing comprehensive information about your AWS costs and usage.

The AWS Cost and Usage Report lists AWS usage for each service category used by an account and its IAM users in hourly or daily details, as well as any tags that you have activated for expense allocation purposes. You can likewise customize the AWS Cost and Usage Report to aggregate your usage information to the every day or month to month level.

Reserved Instance (RI) Reporting

AWS gives various RI-explicit cost the board arrangements out-of-the-case to help you better understand and manage your RIs. Using the RI Utilization and Coverage reports available in AWS Cost Explorer, you can imagine your RI data at a total level or assess a particular RI membership. To access the most detailed RI information accessible, you can use the AWS Cost and Usage Report. You can likewise set a custom RI utilization target via AWS Budgets and get cautions when your usage drops below the threshold you characterize.

Blockchain

Amazon Managed Blockchain

Amazon Managed Blockchain is a completely oversaw service that makes it easy to create and oversee scalable blockchain networks using the popular open source structures Hyperledger Fabric and Ethereum.

Blockchain makes it possible to construct applications where different parties can execute exchanges without the need for a trusted, central authority. Today, building a versatile blockchain network with existing innovations is complex to set up and hard to manage. To make a blockchain network, each network member needs to physically provision hardware, install software, make and manage certificates for access control, and design organizing components. Once the blockchain network is running, you need to continuously screen the infrastructure and adapt to changes, such as a increase in transaction re□uests, or new individuals joining or leaving the network.

Amazon Managed Blockchain is a fully overseen service that allows you to set up and manage an adaptable blockchain arrange with only a couple of snaps. Amazon Managed Blockchain wipes out the overhead required to make the network, and automatically scales to meet the requests of thousands of applications running a great many transactions. Once your system is up and running, Managed Blockchain makes it easy to manage and maintain your blockchain arrange. It manages your certificates, lets you effectively welcome new individuals to join the arrange, and tracks operational metrics such as usage of compute, memory, and capacity resources. In addition, Managed Blockchain can imitate an immutable copy of your blockchain network activity into Amazon Quantum Ledger Database (QLDB), a completely overseen record database. This allows you to easily analyze the network activity outside the network and gain insights into trends.

Business Applications

Alexa for Business

Alexa for Business is an assistance that enables organizations and representatives to use Alexa to get more work done. With Alexa for Business, employees can use Alexa as their intelligent assistant to be more beneficial in meeting rooms, at their work areas, and even with the Alexa gadgets they already have at home.

Amazon WorkDocs

Amazon WorkDocs is a fully managed, secure endeavor storage and sharing service with solid managerial controls and feedback capabilities that improve client productivity.

Users can comment on files, send them to others for criticism, and upload new forms without having to resort to messaging multiple variants of their records as connections. Clients can take advantage of these capacities wherever they are, using the device of their choice, including PCs, Macs, tablets, and phones. Amazon WorkDocs offers IT administrators the option of coordinating with existing corporate directories, adaptable sharing strategies and control of the location where information is put away. You can get started utilizing Amazon WorkDocs with a 30-day free trial providing 1 TB of storage per user for up to 50 users.

Amazon WorkMail

Amazon WorkMail is a secure, oversaw business email and calendar service with support for existing desktop and mobile email client applications. Amazon WorkMail gives users the capacity to flawlessly access their email, contacts, and calendars utilizing the client application of their decision, including Microsoft Outlook, native iOS and Android email applications, any client application supporting the IMAP protocol, or legitimately through a web browser. You can incorporate Amazon WorkMail with your existing corporate directory, use email journaling to meet compliance necessities, and control both the keys that encrypt your data and the location in which your data is put away. You can also set up interoperability with Microsoft Exchange Server, and programmatically oversee users, groups, and resources utilizing the Amazon WorkMail SDK.

Amazon Chime

Amazon Chime is a communications service that changes online meetings with a secure, easy-to-use application that you can trust. Amazon Chime works seamlessly crosswise over your gadgets so that you can stay connected. You can use Amazon Chime for online gatherings, video conferencing, calls, chat, and to share content, both inside and outside your organization.

Amazon Chime works with Alexa for Business, which means you can use Alexa to start your meetings with your voice. Alexa can start your video meetings in large conference rooms, and automatically dial into online gatherings in smaller huddle rooms and from your desk.

Database

Amazon Aurora

Amazon Aurora is a MySQL and PostgreSQL good relational database engine that joins the speed and accessibility of top of the line business databases with the straightforwardness and cost-effectiveness of open source databases.

Amazon Aurora is up to multiple times faster than standard MySQL databases and three times faster than standard PostgreSQL databases. It gives the security, availability, and reliability of commercial databases at 1/tenth the cost. Amazon Aurora is completely overseen by Amazon Relational Database Service (RDS), which robotizes tedious organization errands like equipment provisioning, database setup, fixing, and reinforcements.

Amazon Aurora features a distributed, fault-tolerant, self-healing storage system that auto-scales up to 64TB per database occurrence. It conveys high performance and availability with up to 15 low-latency read replicas, point-in-time recovery, continuous reinforcement to Amazon S3, and replication crosswise over three Availability Zones (AZs).

Amazon RDS

Amazon Relational Database Service (Amazon RDS) makes it easy to set up, operate, and scale a social database in the cloud. It gives cost-proficient and resizable capacity while mechanizing time-consuming administration tasks such as hardware provisioning, database setup, patching and backups. It liberates you to focus on your applications so you can give them the fast execution, high availability, security and similarity they need.

Amazon RDS is available on a few database instance types - upgraded for memory, performance or I/O - and provides you with six familiar database motors to choose from, including Amazon Aurora, PostgreSQL, MySQL, MariaDB, Oracle Database, and SQL Server. You can use the AWS Database Migration Service to effectively move or replicate your existing databases to Amazon RDS.

Amazon RDS on VMware

Amazon Relational Database Service (RDS) on VMware lets you convey managed databases in on-premises VMware environments using the Amazon RDS technology enjoyed by hundreds of thousands of AWS clients. Amazon RDS gives cost-efficient and resizable capacity while computerizing time-consuming administration tasks including equipment provisioning, database setup, fixing, and backups, freeing you to focus on your applications. RDS on VMware brings these same benefits to your on-premises deployments, making it easy to set up, operate, and scale databases in VMware vSphere private information centers, or to migrate them to AWS. RDS on VMware allows you to use the same simple interface for overseeing databases in on-premises VMware environments as you would use in AWS. You can easily repeat RDS on VMware databases to RDS instances in AWS, empowering low-cost cross breed arrangements for disaster recovery, read replica bursting, and discretionary long haul backup retention in Amazon Simple Storage Service (Amazon S3).

Amazon DynamoDB

Amazon DynamoDB is a key-value and document database that conveys single-digit millisecond performance at any scale. It's a completely oversaw, multiregion, multimaster database with worked in security, reinforcement and restore, and in-memory caching for web scale applications. DynamoDB can handle more than 10 trillion re🞐uests per day and support peaks of more than 20 million demands per second.

Many of the world's fastest growing businesses such as Lyft, Airbnb, and Redfin as well as endeavors such as Samsung, Toyota, and Capital One rely upon the scale and execution of DynamoDB to support their main goal basic workloads.

More than 100,000 AWS customers have picked DynamoDB as their key-value and document database for mobile, web, gaming, ad tech, IoT, and other applications that need low-latency information access at any scale. Create another table for your application and let DynamoDB handle the rest.

Amazon ElastiCache

Amazon ElastiCache is a web service that makes it simple to deploy, operate, and scale an in-memory store in the cloud. The administration improves the presentation of web applications by allowing you to retrieve information from fast, managed, in-memory caches, rather of depending entirely on slower disk-based databases.

Amazon ElastiCache supports two open-source in-memory caching motors:

• Redis - a quick, open source, in-memory information store and cache. Amazon ElastiCache for Redis is a Redis-perfect in-memory service that delivers the ease-of-use and control of Redis along with the availability, reliability, and execution appropriate for the most requesting applications. Both single-node and up to 15-

shard bunches are available, enabling scalability to up to 3.55 TiB of in-memory information. ElastiCache for Redis is fully managed, adaptable, and secure. This makes it an ideal up-and-comer to control high-performance use cases such as web, portable apps, gaming, ad-tech, and IoT.

• Memcached - a broadly adopted memory object caching system. ElastiCache for Memcached is protocol compliant with Memcached, so famous tools that you use today with existing Memcached environments will work seamlessly with the service.

Amazon Neptune

Amazon Neptune is a fast, solid, fully-managed chart database service that makes it easy to build and run applications that work with highly connected datasets. The core of Amazon Neptune is a purpose-built, high-performance graph database engine optimized for putting away billions of relationships and questioning the diagram with milliseconds latency. Amazon Neptune supports well known graph models Property Graph and W3C's RDF, and their respective ?uery languages Apache TinkerPop Gremlin and SPARQL, allowing you to effectively build questions that proficiently explore highly connected datasets. Neptune powers graph use cases such as recommendation engines, misrepresentation detection, knowledge graphs, medicate disclosure, and arrange security.

Amazon Neptune is highly available, with read replicas, point-in-time recovery, persistent backup to Amazon S3, and replication across Availability Zones. Neptune is secure with support for encryption at rest. Neptune is fully-managed, so you no longer need to stress over database management tasks such as hardware provisioning, programming patching, setup, configuration, or reinforcements.

Amazon Quantum Ledger Database (QLDB)

Amazon QLDB is a completely managed ledger database that provides a transparent, immutable, and cryptographically certain transaction log owned by a central trusted authority. Amazon QLDB tracks each and every application information change and maintains a complete and certain history of changes over time.

Ledgers are typically used to record a history of economic and monetary action in a organization. Many organizations fabricate applications with ledger-like functionality because they want to maintain an exact history of their applications' data, for instance, following the history of credits and debits in banking transactions, verifying the information lineage of an insurance guarantee, or tracing movement of an item in a supply chain network. Ledger applications are often implemented using custom audit tables or review trails created in relational databases. However, building review functionality with relational databases is time-consuming and prone to human error. It requires custom development, and since social databases are not inherently permanent, any unintended changes to the information are hard to track and verify. Alternatively, blockchain frameworks, such as Hyperledger Fabric and Ethereum, can also be used as a ledger. However, this adds complexity as you need to set-up an entire blockchain organize with various nodes, manage its infrastructure, and require the nodes to validate each transaction before it can be added to the ledger.

Amazon QLDB is another class of database that eliminates the need to engage in the complex development exertion of building your own record like applications. With

QLDB, your information's change history is immutable - it cannot be altered or deleted - and utilizing cryptography, you can easily check that there have been no unintended adjustments to your application's data. QLDB utilizes an immutable transactional log, known as a journal, that tracks each application data change and keeps up a total and verifiable history of changes over time. QLDB is anything but difficult to use because it provides developers with a familiar SQL-like API, an adaptable document information model, and full help for exchanges. QLDB is likewise serverless, so it automatically scales to support the demands of your application. There are no servers to oversee and no read or compose limits to arrange. With QLDB, you only pay for what you use.

Amazon Timestream

Amazon Timestream is a fast, scalable, fully managed time series database administration for IoT and operational applications that makes it easy to store and analyze trillions of occasions per day at 1/tenth the cost of relational databases. Driven by the rise of IoT gadgets, IT frameworks, and keen industrial machines, time-arrangement data — information that measures how things change over time — is one of the fastest growing information types. Time-series data has explicit characteristics such as normally arriving in time order form, information is append-only, and ⃞ueries are always over a time interval. While relational databases can store this information, they are inefficient at processing this information as they lack advancements such as putting away and recovering information by time intervals. Timestream is a purpose-built time series database that effectively stores and processes this data by time intervals. With Timestream, you can without much of a stretch store and analyze log data for DevOps, sensor data for IoT applications, and modern telemetry data for hardware maintenance. As your data grows over time, Timestream's adaptive query processing engine understands its area and design, making your data simpler and faster to analyze. Timestream likewise robotizes rollups, retention, tiering, and compression of data, so you can manage your data at the lowest possible cost. Timestream is serverless, so there are no servers to manage. It manages tedious undertakings such as server provisioning, software fixing, setup, configuration, or information retention and tiering, liberating you to center around building your applications.

Desktop and App Streaming

Amazon WorkSpaces

Amazon WorkSpaces is a fully managed, secure cloud desktop service. You can use Amazon WorkSpaces to provision either Windows or Linux work areas in just a couple minutes and quickly scale to give thousands of desktops to laborers across the globe. You can pay either monthly or hourly, just for the WorkSpaces you launch, which helps you save money when compared to traditional desktops and on-premises VDI arrangements. Amazon

WorkSpaces helps you eliminate the intricacy in managing hardware inventory, OS renditions and patches, and Virtual Desktop Infrastructure (VDI), which helps simplify your work area delivery strategy. With Amazon WorkSpaces, your users get a fast, responsive desktop of their decision that they can access anywhere, whenever, from any upheld device.

Amazon AppStream 2.0

Amazon AppStream 2.0 is a fully oversaw application streaming service. You midway manage your desktop applications on AppStream 2.0 and securely deliver them to any computer. You can without much of a stretch scale to any number of users across the globe without ac uiring, provisioning, and operating equipment or infrastructure.

AppStream 2.0 is built on AWS, so you benefit from a data center and network architecture intended for the most security-sensitive associations. Each client has a liquid and responsive experience with your applications, including GPU-concentrated 3D plan and designing ones, because your applications keep running on virtual machines (VMs) enhanced for specific use cases and each gushing session naturally modifies to network conditions.

Enterprises can use AppStream 2.0 to simplify application delivery and complete their migration to the cloud. Educational institutions can provide every student access to the applications they need for class on any computer. Programming vendors can use AppStream 2.0 to deliver trials, demos, and training for their applications with no downloads or establishments. They can also develop a full software-as-a-service (SaaS) solution without reworking their application.